During the spring of 1997, more than 500 photographers from across the nation were invited to shoot and submit images that captured the heart of Sunday in America.

In response, as a result of a tremendous effort on the part of these photographers, over 5,000 images were received by the editors of Sunday in America. It quickly became apparent that what had been submitted was more than just strikingly high quality images. These individuals had captured, on film and in story, the spirit of Sunday.

After many hours of editing, over 150 images from 75 photographers were selected, powerfully communicating the very qualities that make this day so special and celebrating what makes America truly great:

Faith and Family.

Photograph by David Harrison

Sunday
in America

75 Photographers Celebrate Faith and Family

ZondervanPublishingHouse
A Division of HarperCollinsPublishers

A Tehabi Book

Sunday in America

Copyright © 1997 by Tehabi Books.

Requests for information should be addressed to: Zondervan Publishing House, Grand Rapids, Michigan 49530 http://www.zondervan.com

Sunday in America was developed and produced by Tehabi Books, Del Mar, California. http://www.tehabi.com

Nancy Cash	*Managing Editor*
Mo Latimer	*Project Coordinator*
Laura Georgakakos	*Manuscript Editor*
Jeff Campbell	*Copy Proofer*
Sarah Morgans	*Editorial Assistant*
Sam Lewis	*Webmaster*
Andy Lewis	*Art Director*
Tom Lewis	*Editorial and Design Director*
Sharon Lewis	*Controller*
Chris Capen	*President*

Library of Congress Cataloging-in-Publication Data

Sunday in America : 75 photographers celebrate faith and family.

p. cm.

"A Tehabi Book."

Includes bibliographical references.

ISBN: 0-310-41060-6

1. Christianity —United States. 2. Family—Religious aspects—Christianity. 3. United States—Religious life and customs. 4. Christianity—United States —Pictorial Works 5. Family—Religious aspects—Christianity—Pictorial works. 6. United States—Religious life and customs—Pictorial works.

BR517.S86 1997

277.3'08290222—dc21

97-22578

CIP

This edition is printed on acid-free paper that meets the American National Standards Institute Z39.48 Standard.

Printed in Korea. First edition 1997

97 98 99 00 01 02 03 04 / 10 9 8 7 6 5 4 3 2 1

Pages 2/3: Families gather late on a Sunday afternoon to listen to the sounds of the Dallas Symphony Orchestra at the Dallas Arboretum in White Rock Lake, Texas.

Photograph by Pat Davison

Opposite title page: Solitary prayer at St. Benedict the Moor Church in Pittsburgh, a church that was founded over a century ago in 1889. St. Benedict, the largest African American Catholic church in Pittsburgh, Pennsylvania, stands on a spot known as Freedom Corner. Since the early 1960s, this was the gathering site for every Civil Rights march, and as such, the corner has become a revered landmark in the local Civil Rights Movement.

Photograph by Pat Davison

Contents

Celebrating Sunday

IN FAITH AND FAMILY

M y spiritual journey began many years ago in a Carolina home where Sunday was the Lord's Day, reserved for acts of mercy and necessity, and the gospel was as much a part of our lives as fried chicken, and azaleas in the spring.

My grandmother, Mom Cathey, who lived within two weeks of her one hundredth birthday, was my role model. I remember many Sunday afternoons with other neighborhood children in her home—the lemonade and cookies (I think that was what enticed us), the Bible games, listening to Mom Cathey as she read from her Bible, now one of my most cherished possessions.

She practiced what she preached and lived her life for others. In a tragic accident, Mom lost a son at the hands of a drunk driver. The insurance policy on his life built a hospital wing in a far-off church mission in Pakistan. Although Mom was not at all a wealthy woman, almost anything she could spare went to ministers at home and missions abroad. And when it became necessary in her nineties to go into a nursing home, she welcomed the opportunity.

I can still hear her saying, "Elizabeth, there might be

some people there who don't know the Lord, and I can read the Bible to them."

I love to find her notes in the margins of her Bible, notes written in the middle of the night when she couldn't sleep. For example, I find by Psalm 139 this notation: "May 11, 1952, 1:00 A.M. My prayer: Search me O God and know my heart; try me and know my thoughts. And see if there be any wicked way in me, and lead me in the way everlasting."

I can't remember an unkind word escaping Mom's lips in all the years I knew her, or an ungracious deed marring her path. My grandmother was an almost perfect role model. And I wanted to be like her.

From an early age, I had an active church life. But as we move along, how often in our busy lives something becomes a barrier to total commitment of one's life to the Lord! In some cases, it may be money, power, or prestige.

In my case, my career became of paramount importance. I worked very hard to excel, to achieve. I was really competing against myself, not others. My goal was to do my best, which is all fine and well, but I am inclined to be a perfectionist. And it's very hard to try to control everything, surmount every difficulty, foresee every problem, and realize every opportunity. It can be pretty tough on your family, your friends, your fellow workers, and on yourself. In my case, it began crowding out what Mom Cathey had taught me were life's more important priorities.

I was blessed with a Christian upbringing, a beautiful marriage, and a challenging career. And yet gradually, over many years, I realized what was missing—my life was threatened with spiritual starvation.

I prayed about it, and I believe, no faster than I was ready, God led me to people and circumstances that made a real difference in my life. I found a tremendously caring pastor who helped me see what joy there can be when God is the center of life, and all else flows from that center.

Prayer and fellowship gave me renewed strength as I began to meet each Monday night with others who shared my need to stretch and grow spiritually. And I was strengthened through Bible study with other Senate wives.

I learned that Sundays can be set aside for spiritual and personal rejuvenation without disastrous effect on one's work week. It's on Sundays, when I spend time with my family and with others who set aside time to gather in worship, that I am reminded of those foundational values and priorities I learned at the loving side of Mom Cathey.

When Jesus set out to build the church, He didn't call in a building contractor. He called twelve very human beings together and gave them a job to do. The truth is, it's through relationships, rather than any other means, that God accomplishes the five key elements of what He intends the church to be: a place to celebrate His presence, a community for us to belong to, a real and practical means for needs to be met, an environment where we may grow and develop into the people God designed us to be, and a vehicle to communicate His love to all.

Sunday in America weaves together these foundational purposes and shows how faith and family become the cornerstones of our lives. In this collection of images and writings, I think you may actually see glimpses of yourself, something reminiscent of your best friend, or maybe something that reminds you of your neighbor. God has given us a larger family to belong to. For me, the delight of *Sunday in America* was discovering that beneath the elements that make each of us unique is the essence of what we have in common.

As I've traveled across this great nation, and talked with people from every state, I've found that what continues to hold us together, despite all our diversity, is the unity we share in our faith. In a time when so much focus is being placed on what divides us, *Sunday in America* is a welcome and wonder-filled celebration of how significant our faith and our families really are. ✠

A little boy gets a boost from his father to see what's going on at a March for Jesus event held on Palm Sunday in Austin, Texas. March for Jesus is a nationwide movement committed to sharing the good news about Jesus Christ across America.

Photograph by Kevin Vandivier

Lauren Mannix, Anna Zapata, and Julia Knipp at Lake Highlands United Methodist Church in Dallas, Texas, receive their first Bibles traditionally given to third graders during a special autumn service.

Photograph by Louis DeLuca

Dimnent Chapel, at Hope College, became an anchor to the community in Holland, Michigan, on Sunday, December 7, 1941, just hours after the attack on Pearl Harbor. On that day, what was planned as a Christmas vesper service became a time of shared concern and prayerful petition on behalf of America, and a lasting memorial to those who had lost their lives. Today, over 4,000 people attend this service on the first Sunday of Advent each year.

Photograph by John deVisser

Members of the St. James Episcopal Children's Choir make their way down the aisle at a pace much faster than the music. The church is located in Skaneateles, New York.

Photograph by Tom Watson

Children raise arms and voices in song and celebration at Saddleback Valley Community Church, a congregation of 12,000 worshipers in Mission Viejo, California.

Photograph by Bruce C. Strong

▲ *Thirty thousand people rose early and gathered at the Red*

Rocks amphitheatre, near Morrison, Colorado, to celebrate the

resurrection of Jesus on this Easter morn.

Photograph by Matthew Lester

The absence of wind didn't discourage Sean Cook ▶
from heading out to Zilker Park in Austin, Texas, to fly his
kite on a Sunday afternoon. He just hopped on his bike and
pedaled up some wind of his own.

Photograph by Kevin Vandivier

▲

Pete Bowell and Emily Cook exchange smiles while

swinging during a pleasant Sunday afternoon in front of the

Cook's home in Lanexa, Virginia.

Photograph by Al Cook

▲

David basks in the warmth of the sun and of his father's

love as they playfully enjoy a priceless moment at Belgrade

Lakes, near Augusta, Maine. A few years ago, after

growing tired of the hectic and demanding pace of a well-

paying job, Jeff Bass decided to move with his family to

Mission Hill. One of his motivations for change was the

desire to spend more time with his family,

where he finds strength and refreshment

from his wife and two sons.

Photograph by Dorothy Littell Greco

▲ Sunday chores at the Gay home in Smyrna, Georgia.

Fifteen-year-old Brooke does the dishes while her brother

takes out the trash.

Photograph by Rob Nelson

Joe Norman was never close to his father. ▲

Now that he's a father, he's especially determined to have a

strong relationship with his children, Jourdan and Alexander.

"I want to give them something to hold on to."

Photograph by Pat Davison

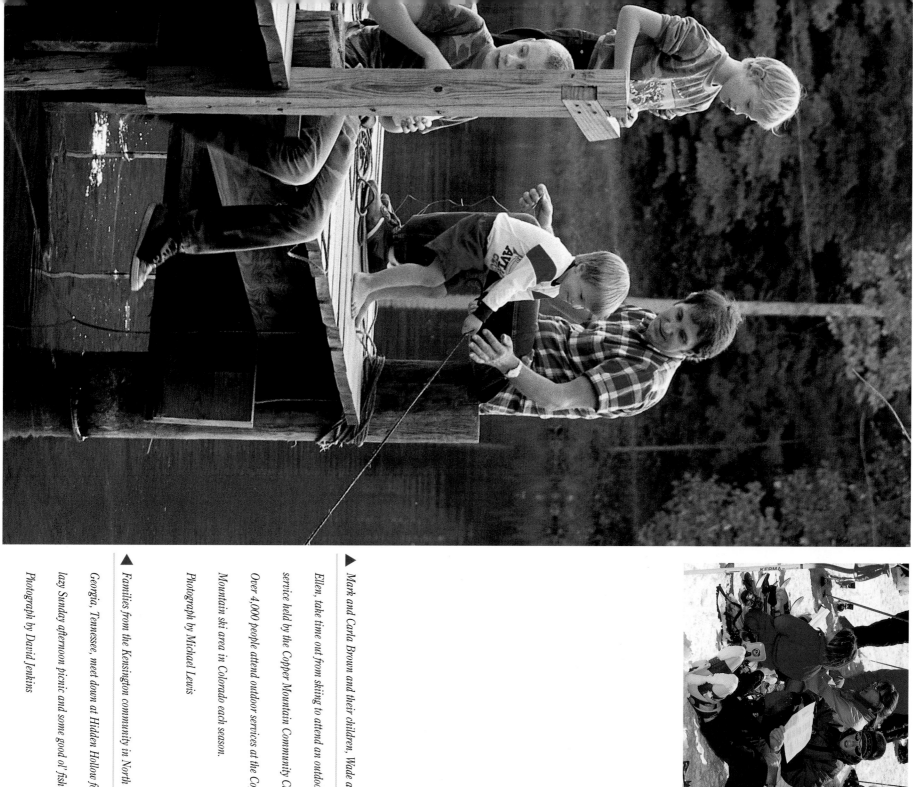

▶ *Mark and Carla Brown and their children, Wade and Ellen, take time out from skiing to attend an outdoor service held by the Copper Mountain Community Church. Over 4,000 people attend outdoor services at the Copper Mountain ski area in Colorado each season.*

Photograph by Michael Lewis

▲ *Families from the Kensington community in North Georgia, Tennessee, meet down at Hidden Hollow for a lazy Sunday afternoon picnic and some good ol' fishing.*

Photograph by David Jenkins

 *Emma Fulford manages to convince her dad, Robert,*

to sneak off with her for a little exploration while the rest of

the family celebrates Easter morning at an outdoor service

held on the grounds of the equestrian stadium in

Coto de Caza, California.

Photograph by Bruce C. Strong

Every Sunday in the spring, during the month before Easter, ▶
Grandma and Grandpa Jernigan fix lunch for their extended
family and have a small Easter egg hunt out in the yard for
all their grandkids. The kids love finding the treats and
Grandma and Grandpa think having all the grandchildren
over is quite a treat as well! Galen Jernigan pauses for a
moment to check out the horizon for any other goodies.

Photograph by Doug Hopfer

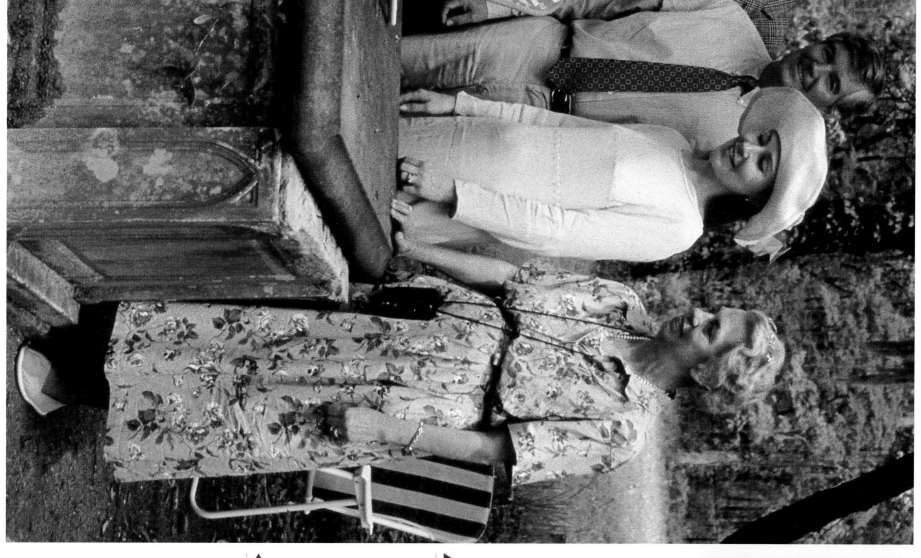

▶ Singers at New Prospect United Presbyterian Church, just

outside Beckville, Texas, gather for "Dinner on the Grounds"

after a Sacred Harp session, an old Southern tradition of

participatory choral music, often led by itinerate teachers.

Photograph by Randy Mallory

▲ Four generations of the Jackson family gather at a

graveside amid the ruins of the Old Sheldon Church—

a church built before the American Revolution—following

a memorial service held annually since 1923 by

St. Helena's Episcopal Church in Beaufort, South Carolina.

After the service, families picnic under the spreading oak

branches among headstones that date back to the 1750s.

Photograph by Rick Harrig

Attendees at Saddleback Community Church in California

are sure to be welcomed on a Sunday morning by

Rick Muchow and the upbeat sounds

of the Saddleback Singers and Orchestra.

Since beginning in 1980 with two families,

Saddleback's congregation has grown to over 12,000

under the leadership of Pastor Rick Warren (center stage),

and has sponsored the planting

of twenty-four "daughter" churches.

Photographs by Bruce C. Strong

▲ *Every fall in downtown Garland, Texas, the community*

celebrates the autumn season with a family festival of

music, games, and fun. This little angel was collecting

prizes just as quickly as she could.

Photograph by Louis DeLuca

Grateful hearts and exuberant voices

lead the congregation Sunday morning at the

First Institutional Baptist Church in Phoenix, Arizona.

Photograph by Ron Londen ▲

▲ Six-year-old Andrea Edwards keeps her eye on the choir

director as the children of Lake Highlands United Methodist

Church in Dallas, Texas, perform during

the morning service.

Photograph by Louis DeLuca

The family of Pastor Richard Haney worships ▲

together at the Swift Creek Presbyterian Church

on the outskirts of Richmond, Virginia.

On this day, the Haney family, Charlotte, Pam, and

Leah, celebrates a visit from Richard's father, Glenn,

while the congregation celebrates the move

to a new church home after six years of meeting for

worship in a local movie theatre.

Photograph by Al Cook

Reaching Up
IN WORSHIP

God stretched out the heavens, stippling the night with impressionistic stars. He set the sun to the rhythm of the day, the moon to the rhythm of the month, the seasons to the rhythm of the year. He blew wind through reedy marshes and beat drums of distant thunder. He formed a likeness of Himself from a lump of clay and into it breathed life. He crafted a counterpart to complete the likeness, joining the two halves and placing them center stage in His creation where there was a temptation and a fall, a great loss and a great hiding. God searched for the hiding couple, reaching to pick them up, dust them off, and draw them near. Though they hardly knew it at the time. . . . He searched for their children and for their children's children. And afterward wrote stories of His search. . . .

God gave us art, music, sculpture, drama, and literature . . . as footpaths to lead us out of our hiding places and as signposts to lead us along in our search for what was lost. . . .

We reach for God in many ways. Through our sculptures and our Scriptures. Through our pictures and our prayers. Through our writing and our worship.

And through them He reaches us. ‡

▲ *J. R. White and his son, John, pray together at a Promise Keepers Conference in New Orleans. Promise Keepers is a Christ-centered outreach ministry dedicated to uniting men and equipping them to become godly influences. Men are encouraged to make and keep basic promises of commitment to God, to their families, and to their fellow man.*

Photograph by Louis DeLuca.

▲ *Members of the Peaceful Rest Missionary Baptist Church*

join in prayer. Peaceful Rest was one of a chain of churches

linking the small community known as Freedman's Town,

originally the site of slave quarters and the first place in Texas

to hear the news of the Emancipation Proclamation.

Photograph by James Frederick Housel

Andriana Kolendrianos leads the Saint Barbara Greek ▶
Orthodox Choir in songs of praise from high above the
congregation as they gather to celebrate the resurrection of
the Lord Jesus during an Easter candlelight
service in Santa Barbara, California.

Photograph by Rina Ganassa

▲ *The New Life Community Choir of Durham, North Carolina,*

performs a gospel concert on Homecoming weekend at

Delaware State University.

Photograph by Brian Branch-Price

▲ John P. Kee (far right) performs at a

concert in Dover, Delaware. The group, known for its

Christian gospel rock music, has gained notoriety

for its "Praise" performances.

Photograph by Brian Branch-Price

▶ Dozens of gospel greats participate in a studio recording session in Alexandria, Indiana, led by Bill Gaither at the piano.

Photograph by Rob Nelson

▲ The lead singer, Jason Wesson, of the contemporary Christian rock band "Between Thieves" reaches up in worship during a performance in the Dallas area.

Photograph by Louis DeLuca

Because of His Love

BY TONY EVANS

The God most of us worship is too small. The God of most Christians seems anemic, weak, and limited. He does not have the capacity to make a difference, to turn things around. The God most of us serve resembles more the flickering of a candle than the burning of the noonday sun.

One reason for this is that we do not understand God's sovereignty. We have allowed God to be everywhere but on the throne, and we have paid dearly in our own spiritual failure and weakness and limited power because the God we talk about has little to do with the sovereign God of the universe.

God's sovereignty concerns his absolute rule and control over all of His creation. God rules absolutely over the affairs of men. He sits on the throne of the universe as Lord. Everything that happens comes about because He either directly causes it or consciously allows it. Nothing enters into history or could even exist outside of history that does not come under the complete control of God.

Only when you understand that this is the kind of God with whom we have to deal will you take seriously the issue of His authority. I know that many people do not like the doctrine of God's sovereignty. They don't want a sovereign God. Certainly non-Christians, and unfortunately many times we as Christians, don't want a sovereign God because we don't want anyone ruling over us. We want to be autonomous. . . .

But once you understand God's sovereignty, you realize nobody can be autonomous from Him. You and I function in a universe over which He has absolute control by causing or allowing everything. When we know that kind of God, it will graphically change the way we think, act, and live.

The sovereignty of God means that He exercises His prerogative to do whatever He pleases with His creation. God can do whatever He wants to do simply because it's all His. "The earth is the Lord's, and all it contains, the world, and those who dwell in it" (Ps. 24:1). By virtue of His ownership, God can do whatever He wants to do whenever He wants to do it. . . .

Not even evil and unrighteousness can escape the all-controlling hand of God. I love Revelation 19:6, which says,

"For the Lord our God, the Almighty, reigns." God rules! Even when it looks like He's not ruling, He's ruling. When chaos appears, He's ruling the chaos. When things are falling apart, He's ruling the falling apart of those things.

Our God is sovereign. That means there's no such thing as luck. The word ought to be expunged from the dictionary, or at least from any serious usage. You are never lucky or unlucky. Under God, no chance happenings occur. Anything that happens to you, good or bad, must pass through His fingers first. There are no accidents with God. . . .

Not the smallest detail of our lives escapes Him—*none*. That creates a problem for us because the question must now be answered: If in fact God is this kind of God, then why do my decisions matter? If He is sovereign and has already determined everything that will happen according to what pleases Him, then why do I need to choose? Why not just sit back, relax, and let Him do what He's doing since He's going to do it anyway? . . .

I don't propose to have the last word on the subject; however, I do have a word on it. Suppose I were to go downtown in Dallas, with my destination being city hall. That is my determined purpose, but I am not limited to just one option for getting there. I could take the direct route to downtown Dallas by jumping on Interstate 35 and arriving at my destination.

However, for one reason or another I may choose not to go that route. That choice will in no way impede me from getting to city hall because I know at least two other courses. While my goal remains the same, I can keep my options open.

God has determined in His sovereign will where He's going to wind up. But within the context of His will, He has many ways of getting there. He allows you to make choices. Your choices will not determine whether God winds up where He wants to go. He will arrive at His destination, but your choices affect which route He takes. God is going to get there either through you, around you, over you, by you, or in spite of you. When it is all said and done, however, even the route you choose will be the one He sovereignly planned to use in order to achieve His intended purposes.

You get to participate in choosing the route God takes. Does He run over you? Does He remove you? Does He bless you? Does He curse you? You will not stop God from getting where He wants to go. The question is, how will you look once He arrives? . . .

What about prayer? God has determined what He's going to do, but He will not do certain things until we make the choice to pray. "You do not have because you do not ask" (James 4:2). It is like a mother who has a very sick child. She knows when she puts the child to bed that she's going to have to get up in the middle of the night to minister to the child, and she determines to do so.

Sherri Sperling and her son, Brad, join in worship with their church family at the Reynoldsburg United Methodist Church in Columbus, Ohio.

Photograph by James D. DeCamp

But she won't get up until the child calls out. The child's call does not make the mother do something. She had already decided she was going to do it, but in her sovereign choice she decided not to do it until the child called. So when she hears "Mama," the mother will do what she had already planned to do. . . .

So God has given us options within His sovereignty to determine how we will fit into the outworking of His sovereignty. No one will thwart the plan of God. All we can do is cooperate with it. . . .

You exist for God. That is why you were created. You were not made just to get a good job, to live happily ever after, to get married, and to have kids. Those you call bonuses. You were created to bring God glory and to accomplish His purposes on earth. That's why you will find no rest in life until you find your rest in Him. . . .

Since God is sovereign, why did He allow the existence and proliferation of evil, especially in light of the fact that God hates sin (Rom. 1:18), is completely holy (Isa. 6:3), and cannot sin (Ps. 5:4; 1 John 1:13)? . . . First of all, since God does everything for His glory (Eph. 1:11–12), we must naturally conclude that God will get more glory with the existence of sin than without it. This makes sense because some of God's attributes are most clearly demonstrated against a backdrop of sin. The greatness of His love shows most clearly in contrast to our sinfulness (Rom. 5:8). God's holiness and wrath, two indispensable aspects of His nature, could never be fully seen without the reality of sin (Rom. 1:18; 9:22–23). Most important, the magnificence of His grace could hardly be measured except against the ugliness of sin (Eph. 2:1–7). Thus, in allowing sin, the glory of God's attributes and character is most visibly displayed.

Second, in allowing the existence of evil, God is allowing everything that can be attempted to thwart His kingdom so that throughout ages to come, it will be unquestionably clear that no enemy or scheme can succeed against the Almighty One. . . .

Finally, God allows evil because of His love. He does not wish to coerce obedience. For God to coerce obedience would invalidate the authentic nature of that obedience, especially since God looks at the heart (Rom. 8:27), which remains disobedient. In order for man to function authentically as God's image-bearer, which includes functioning as a moral agent with the power to choose, the possibility of evil must exist. For God to have negated that possibility would be for Him to nullify the very thing He created. Personhood would be reduced to robotics.

▲ *Father Joseph Brown, a Jesuit priest, spoke to the people at St. Vincent de Paul Catholic Church in Nashville, Tennessee, during a Lenten season revival. Lent, a season observed by many Christian churches, is a forty-day period prior to Easter, where sin or wrongdoing is regretfully acknowledged with a resolve to change.*

Photograph by Randy Piland

We must therefore conclude that God neither causes sin, incites it, authorizes it, or approves it. He does, however, permit it by allowing His creatures, whom He has endowed with a moral will, to rebel against His authority. He then sovereignly overrules their evil to accomplish His sovereign predetermined purposes. In the allowance of evil, God demonstrates how great He really is. . . .

The sovereignty of God should lead us to enthusiastic worship of Him. You know what ought to draw us to church on Sunday? The fact that the sovereign God, who holds up the universe by the word of His power, wants to have a meeting with us; that this great God, who gives us the air we breathe every day, who provides us everything we need, wants to meet with us. . . . Who else can create moons, stars, planets, and other galaxies? Who can create just the right temperature and keep the earth rotating at just the right speed so that it rotates around the sun at just the right season?

Who can give us just the right animals from which we get just the right clothes and the right food? Who can create just the right wood so we can build just the right houses? Who is like our God? He deserves your worship, your homage. He deserves your bowing before His face, glorifying his name. He deserves your passionate worship. ‡

‡ *From Our God Is Awesome by Tony Evans*

45

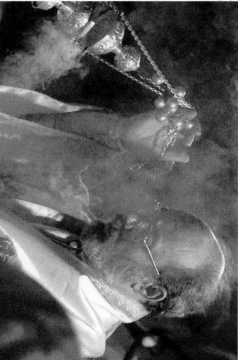

Immersed in clouds of sweet-smelling smoke from his censer,

Archbishop Spyridon prays over the bread and the

wine just prior to Holy Communion at the St. Sophia

Greek Orthodox Cathedral in Washington, D.C.

This was the archbishop's first celebration of the liturgy and

Eucharist at the cathedral after his appointment as the spiritual

head of the Greek Orthodox Church in the United States.

Photograph by Bill Petros

▲ A handful of fresh-picked tulips brightens Easter morning

following services at Avon United Methodist Church in

Mount Vernon, Washington. The Skagit Valley

is a rural area that is world famous for its tulips and

annual tulip festival.

Photograph by Alan Craft

Two-year-old Loriana Magola experiences her first

Christmas Eve in America. Loriana's family, along

with other Ukrainian refugees, found community and

friendship at the First Ukrainian Evangelical

Baptist Church in Philadelphia, Pennsylvania.

Photograph by Home Mission Board,

Southern Baptist Convention

"Tear Down The Walls" was the theme of the Promise Keepers Conference in New Orleans, Louisiana, which was attended by thousands of men.

Photograph by Louis DeLuca

More than 50,000 men share the closing moments of a Promise Keepers Conference on Folsom Field at the University of Colorado. Much more than a series of stadium events, Promise Keepers is a year-round ministry serving men through educational seminars, resource materials, and the local church. From the first event in 1990, attended by seventy-two men, the conference has grown to the stadium-sized events of today attended by more than 2 million men.

Photograph by David Harrison

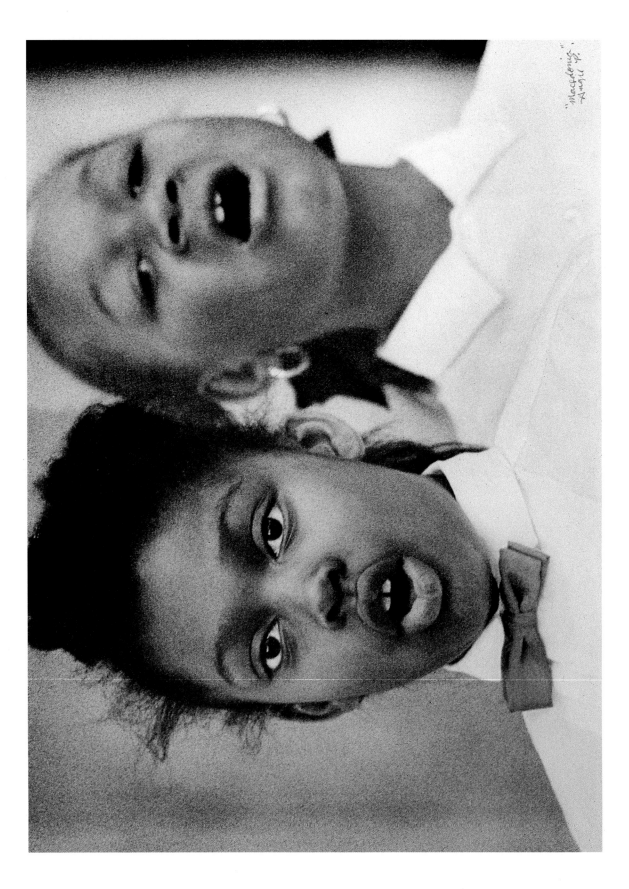

▲ Megan Parker and Veronika Davenport join in song at the

Macedonia Missionary Church in Eatonville, Florida, the oldest

black incorporated town in America. Photographer Angela Peterson

believes the support offered by the church is very important

to African Americans, and to black culture. "It's where we come

together. It's what we know. When all else fails, we have

our God to come to."

Photograph by Angela Peterson

Choir members raise their hands in joyful worship at ▲

Peaceful Rest Missionary Baptist Church, one of the

many local churches that have united their

neighborhood of tiny homes into a rural oasis, an area

of astonishing unity amid the chaos of downtown

Houston, Texas. These churches serve their community

well as havens of support,

entertainment, and moral certainty.

Photograph by James Frederick Housel

▲ *Mrs A. J. McCann plays hymns as members of the Texas*

Cowboy Oldtimers Association gather for a memorial service

in Stamford, Texas, to honor and celebrate those who survived

the frontier's hard times and to remember the days of the open

range. The Texas Cowboy Reunion, which has occured every

July since 1930, includes a parade, a cook-off, country-western

dancing, and a rodeo that draws more than 20,000 visitors

to the fringe of the North Texas grasslands.

Photograph by Doug Milner

Bikers from around the Denver, Colorado area, gather
at the annual "Bikers Sonrise Service," hosted by the
Christian Motorcyclist Association.

Photograph by David Harrison

Something of Significance

BY JONI EARECKSON TADA

bout ten years ago, I was sitting in church one Sunday morning. Our pastor, John McArthur, was off somewhere at a pastor's conference, and we had a guest speaker. Frankly, this man's sermon wasn't holding my interest. I hate to admit it, but I was plain bored.

I suppose I could have let my thoughts wander, but I thought to myself, *Come on, this is the Lord's Day. It's a Sunday morning worship service. I want to do something that honors God. And if I can't get grabbed by this sermon, I'm just going to bring every one of my thoughts under obedience to the Lord Jesus Christ.*

So I decided to pray. But I needed a focus, so my eyes fell on the back of a person's head, a man about five or six pews in front of me. I didn't see his face. I didn't know his name. I didn't even know if he knew Christ, but I decided I would spend the next thirty minutes or so in concentrated prayer for this man, whoever he was. And so I began praying.

O Father in heaven, thank You that You have loved this individual, whoever he is. And God, if he knows You, would You deepen his love for Your Word? And Father, if he doesn't know You, would You have that pastor up there say something of significance about the gospel so he might be brought into your kingdom? Lord, strengthen this man whoever he is.

Father, if he's not married and he is dating somebody, don't let him get away with any sexual immorality. Keep him, hold him to his morals. Lord, if he is married, don't let him cheat on his wedding vows. Keep him honorable, would you, God? Don't let those girls in his office, whoever they are, flirt with him. And don't let him be pulled away by temptation.

I stared at the man's head, his hair black and shining, and a wave of peace washed over me as I sensed victory in prayer. I kept praying.

Strengthen this man, would You, God? Refine his faith, keep him from lies, clean up his bad habits, would You? Assist him in prayer and sustain him in health. Guard his mind, God. Lord, would You deepen his friendships, help him to obey, increase his love for You? Lord, if he is having problems with his mom or dad, resolve those conflicts at home, would You? God, help him to get along with his boss or supervisor at work so he'll be a more honorable witness and testimony to you. Lord, answer his questions,

Baby Andrew seems to raise his hand in response to teacher

Cliff Niemeier in the Palma Smiley program at Southeast

Christian Church in Louisville, Kentucky. The class, designed

for six- to eighteen-month-old children, is a hands-on

learning program named after the woman who

developed it over twenty years ago.

Photograph by Gibbs Frazeur

---

would you, if he has any doubts about his faith.

I prayed on and on. After thirty minutes, I can't tell you how excited I was! I was thrilled that I had prayed for this person I didn't even know. I was worshiping God in this very practical way of being specific.

When the service was over, I thought about making my way down to that man and mentioning my prayer. But no. He'd think I was nuts! Or making advances or something. And I didn't want the morning's victory to be tarnished. I decided to keep my prayer a secret between God and me.

God surprised me with the rest of the story. I met this man about one month after I had prayed for him in church. Introduced by a mutual friend, I noticed a good-looking Oriental guy with broad shoulders and striking black hair. The hair looked familiar, so I said, "Would you turn around a minute and let me see the back of your head?"

I couldn't believe it! I said, "I can't believe this, but I prayed for you for about half an hour in church about a month ago." He really thought I was a little crazy for doing that, but it sparked his interest—he thought I was unusual. We became friends, and he asked me out on a date. To make a long story short, about eighteen months later we married, and I am pleased to be the wife of my wonderful husband, Ken Tada.

When we are specific in prayer, God "is able to do immeasurably more than all we ask or imagine, according to his power that is at work within us" (Eph. 3:20). Isn't that marvelous? God wants to do so much more than we could ever ask. When we buckle down and get specific, our sovereign God will do far more than we could ever imagine.

A few years ago I was invited by the Billy Graham Evangelistic Association to lead two workshops during "Amsterdam '86," a large international congress on Third World evangelism. There were evangelists there from over 160 countries, including Malawi, Bangladesh, India, the Solomon Islands, Western Samoa, and the Philippines. It was incredible!

Our workshops on sharing Christ with those who are disabled were wonderfully well attended. Between sessions, I was almost hit broadside by an excited evangelist with dark olive skin and a bushy beard. In a thick Middle Eastern accent, he said, "Oh, I must tell you that I am from Iran, and I must tell you that my friends and I translated your books into the Persian language and have been sharing them faithfully with handicapped people in Tehran."

It was all I could do not to cry right in front of the man. When I wrote *Joni* and *A Step Farther*, I thought maybe a few disabled people like me, in wheelchairs, could benefit from the message. I figured my relatives might buy a copy. But when that evangelist from Iran told me about a Persian version of my book, it really made me think. I wish I had been a lot more specific in my prayers about the ministry of those books when they were first published. Yet God was doing far more than I could ever ask or even imagine, turning my small, specific request into a grand answer!

Perhaps you remember the story of Jacob wrestling with God. You'll find it in Genesis 32:24–28. Jacob wrestled with God through the night until daybreak, and God touched Jacob's hip so that his hip was wrenched out of its socket. The man said, "Let me go, for it is daybreak."

But Jacob replied, "I will not let you go unless you bless me." Because Jacob persevered, God changed Jacob's name to Israel, because he had "struggled with God and with men and . . . overcome."

Have you struggled with something until you were sure it was God's will? Have you persevered in prayer because you know it is right? Charles Spurgeon said:

"It is delightful to hear a man wrestle with God and say, 'I will not let Thee go except Thou bless me,' but that must be said softly and not in a hectoring spirit, as though we could command and exact blessings from the Lord of all. Remember it is still a man wrestling, even though permitted to wrestle with the eternal *I AM*. Jacob halted on his thigh after that night's holy conflict, to let him see that God is terrible, and that his prevailing power did not lie in himself. We are taught to say, 'Our Father,' but still it is, 'Our Father *who art in heaven*.' Familiarity there may be, but holy familiarity; boldness, but the boldness that springs from grace and is the work of the Spirit; not the boldness of the rebel who carries a brazen font in the presence of his offended king, but the boldness of the child who fears because he loves, and loves because he fears." (*Lectures to My Students*, Charles Haddon Spurgeon)

I like Martin Luther's prayer: "Lord I will have my will of Thee at this time, because I know it is Thy will." Have you ever been able to pray that way? When we are sure what we are asking for is for God's glory, not for selfish gain or impure motives, then we can say with Jacob, "I will not let Thee go except Thou bless me." It's a risky prayer, isn't it? Some people have broken their necks finding God. Other people like Jacob have had their hips thrown out of socket. But ah, the blessings that come! ‡

▲ *Dui Pham waits alongside his mother, Thuc Ng Pham, on the day of his First Holy Communion at Holy Cross Catholic Church in Lansing, Michigan.*

Photograph by Michael Schimpf

‡ *From Seeking God by Joni Eareckson Tada*

56

Paige Glascock from Hannibal, Missouri—best known as

Mark Twain's home town—is also known for her lively

imagination and storytelling abilities: here she waits for her

family after services at Immanuel Baptist Church.

Photograph by Bob Greenlee

▲ *A youth soaks in the sounds of celebration and praise*

at a concert performed by "David and the Giants"

in Holland, Michigan.

Photograph by David Banta

Over 400 attendees at the Ghost Ranch, a year-round education ▶

and mission center of the Presbyterian Church (U.S.A.) that is

located in the mountains of northern New Mexico, gather

outside the Lower Pavilion to participate in Communion on

their eighth and final day at the ranch. People of diverse faiths

and racial and cultural origins participate in over 300

workshops, ranging from anthropology and science to fine arts,

photography, social issues, writing, and spirituality,

which are offered throughout the year.

Photograph by Jonathan A. Meyers

▲ *A proud pair of altar boys look out over the congregation of*

St. Phillips Catholic Church in Detroit, Michigan, before Mass

begins. Boys have long assisted clergy with communion and

processional duties. In the last few years, however, girls have

been allowed to participate in alter service as well.

Photograph by Dwight Cendrowski

▲ Three Taos Pueblo Indian men pause to chat after attending

Mass on a cold January Sunday morning at the San

Gerónimo de Taos Church in northern New Mexico.

The church sits on the site of the original mission.

Photograph by Jonathan A. Meyers

A new member of the Temple of Prayer and

Deliverance Church in Augusta, Georgia, is baptized by

Deacon James Walker during an early-morning

service at the Savannah River.

Deacon James Walker and Reverend Helen Turner

pray for the new members of their church following their

baptism. Reverend Turner's remarkable life has come full

circle: she found new life after early years of prostitution,

drug addiction, and a conviction for attempted murder,

by accepting Christ while in jail.

Photographs by Robert Seale

▲ *Robert Trujillo, with his guitar, and other members of*

Connections, a college fellowship based in Phoenix, Arizona,

come together for a sunrise service

atop Squaw Peak Mountain.

Photograph by Ron Londen

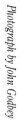 A campfire illuminates tired youth group members of

Wesley Memorial United Methodist Church of Decatur, Alabama.

The students are worshiping together after a day spent

planting a garden at a daycare facility for

Alzheimer's patients in McKenzie, Alabama.

Photograph by John Godbey

Taylor and Chimere Glover, Krystle Triplett, and Brandy

Dotson join in the celebration on Palm Sunday at Holy

Rosary Church, Saint Charles Lwanga parish

in Homewood, Pennsylvania.

Photograph by Robert Pavuchak

▲

Brenda Johnson and her son, Julius III, lift their hands

in prayer in downtown Cleveland, Ohio, during

a National Day of Prayer.

Photograph by Gus Chan

▲

Joining Hands

IN FAMILY

I caught a glimpse one Sunday afternoon of something dear to God.

It should have been a day to push back the papers that cluttered the desk of my soul, but the papers were urgent and I was anxious. I was behind on a writing project with a fast-approaching deadline, so I had set aside Sunday afternoon to spend catching up.

Early that afternoon, though, my daughter asked if I would take her to see a friend who was playing in a roller hockey game. The friend was a boy whom I'll call Joey. He had cerebral palsy, my daughter said, and he had asked her at school Friday if she would come and watch him play. She told him she would if she could get a ride.

As it turned out, I was the only ride available.

I said yes, knowing if I didn't, that something precious would be lost, and though I didn't know what that was, I knew it was greater than whatever could be gained by saying no.

When we arrived at the roller rink, I went in with her, thinking I could find a quiet nook and get some work done. But inside, all kinds of noises echoed off the bare walls and slatted wood floor. Video

Photograph by Mark Williams

▲ *How could you not believe in God with all the beauty around us? Brenda and Doug Milner with their daughter, Sophie, pause during a family hike at Enchanted Rock near Fredericksburg, Texas.*

arcades lined one of the walls, luring young boys with loose change. A concession stand lined another, luring the rest of us. Families of the players milled around, talking, several of them leaning against the perimeter railing.

I was looking for an out-of-the-way place to write, when my daughter pointed out Joey. He was playing goalie, hidden behind shin guards, face mask, and a chest guard. He had been positioned where he didn't have to move much, so I hardly noticed he was handicapped. All I noticed was that he stood a foot taller and years older than the other players.

Gathered at the railing behind Joey were four boys from my daughter's school. She joined them while I nested in a vacant table, taking out my pen and notebook, busying myself with all the catching up I had scheduled for that afternoon. But the sight of those five high school kids and the sound of their cheering distracted me. I stopped and paused and wondered if there was something I should be paying attention to. . . .

Suddenly I realized that there are many ways a person can be impoverished, and sometimes the least of those ways is materially. That was the case with Joey.

His poverty was not material; it was relational. He didn't need money or what money could buy. He needed something it couldn't buy—friends. He needed, as we all need, friends who will talk to him in the hall and sit with him at lunch and have him over to spend the night. He needed, as we all need, friends who will show up at a crosstown roller rink, lean against the railing, and cheer him on. . . .

"If we are to love our neighbors," says Frederick Buechner, "before doing anything else we must *see* our neighbors. With our imagination as well as with our eyes, that is to say like artists, we must see not just their faces but the life behind and within their faces."

▲ *Team members pray with their youth pastor and team captain before a competition that tested their knowledge of Bible verses at the National Youth Convention for the Church of the Nazarene in Orlando, Florida.*

Photograph by Jean-Claude Lejeune

That day I saw something behind the face of the hockey mask and behind the face of cerebral palsy.

I saw Joey.

Besides Joey, I wondered what else there was to see in that roller rink on that Sunday afternoon. I looked beyond him to the five kids still at the railing. They could have been at the video arcade. They could have been at the concession stand. They could have been at the table, talking among themselves, joking among themselves, preoccupied with themselves. And who could blame them if they were? We would be there ourselves, doing the same things ourselves, wouldn't we?

But they weren't there; they were at the railing. They weren't preoccupied with themselves; they were preoccupied with Joey. Watching him. Encouraging him. Cheering him on.

And as they did, something changed hands. What was it? I squinted. A gift of some sort. A gift Joey desperately needed. Neither the hands of the giver nor the hands of the receiver were aware of the exchange. But the Father who sees in secret, He saw it, He took note of it, He treasured it.

And so did I.

A block party—Italian style. Anthony Dema and his family and friends enjoy Sunday lunch in his driveway on 73rd Street in Brooklyn, New York.

Photograph by Ethel Wolovitz

▶ *The Boyd Bailey family, of Woodstock, Georgia, joins*

hands in prayer over Sunday dinner with those members

of the family willing to take part.

Photograph by Rob Nelson

▲ People from the San Francisco Bay Area gather for Sunday celebration at Glide Memorial United Methodist Church. Glide offers innovative and nontraditional programs such as health care, crisis intervention, substance abuse recovery, literacy, and training programs, and it has grown to be one of the most comprehensive nonprofit human service providers in the San Francisco Bay Area.

Photograph by Nita Winter

▲ Jeffrey Skinner, Cliff Berschneider, Carl Smith, and Richard Buzzell join hands to recite the Lord's Prayer during a Sunday Mass at the Holy Rosary Church in Homewood, Pennsylvania.

Photograph by Robert Paruchak

▲ When the Meade Memorial Episcopal Church (a traditionally black church) in

Alexandria, Virginia, needed a place to worship while their sanctuary was

being rebuilt, Father Jack Woodard asked the Church of St. Clement

(a predominantly white church), if they would allow Meade Memorial to use

their building when it was not in use. The people of the Church of St. Clement

declined their request, saying they'd prefer the people of Meade Memorial to join

them at the services and consider St. Clement their home during the building

process. During the first Easter these congregations spent together, photographer

Walter P. Calahan asked permission to take portraits during coffee hour. These

portraits reveal some of the friendships that may have never occurred if these

two churches hadn't joined hands in helping one another grow stronger.

(Top left) Melvin Mobley, Jr., and Paul C. Spiess became good friends while singing

in the choir. (Top center) Anthony D. Lee reacts after Nora B. O'Reilly gave him a

kiss. (Top right) Lucila G. Woodard, the wife of Meade Memorial's rector, the Rev.

Jack Woodard, embraces Jennifer Courtney Young, an acolyte for St. Clement.

(Bottom left) James M. Taylor boosts up Michael Ward, a member of his Sunday

School class. (Bottom center) Rev. Grace Louise Cangialosi, assistant to the rector

of the Church of St. Clement, Rev. Jack Woodard, rector of Meade Memorial

Church, and Rev. Rosemari Sullivan, rector of the Church of St. Clement, clown

around. (Bottom right) Louise B. Keyes holds Joey Connor. Louise remembers

holding many of the present-day mothers of Meade Memorial when they were babies.

Photographs by Walter P. Calahan

77

Every year, folks in Bushnell, Illinois, a tiny farming community in a sea of cornfields, welcome hundreds of youth from all over the country to Cornerstone, a five-day Christian music festival. Teens fill the hours with concerts, art exhibits, workshops, walks in the moonlight, theological discussions, and good clean fun.

Photograph by David Banta

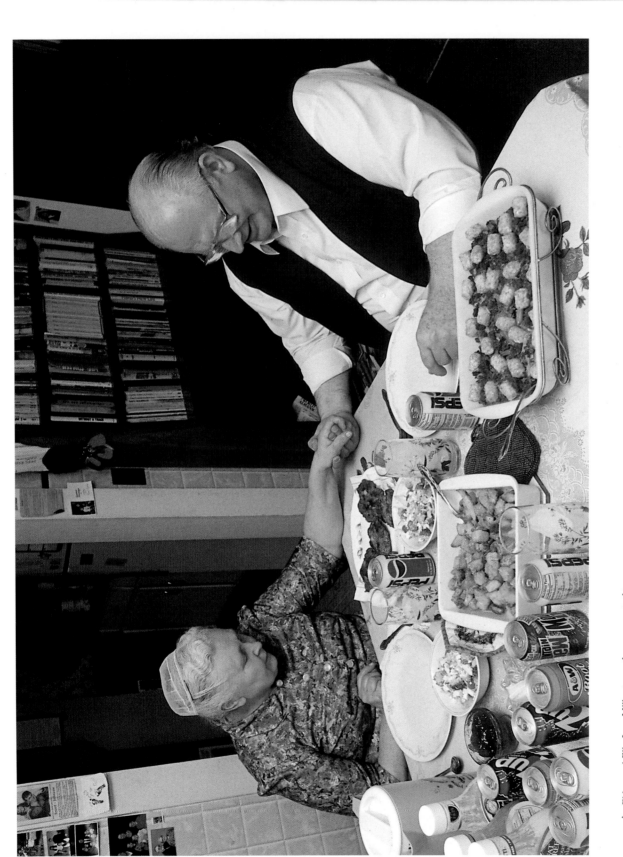

▲ *Eldon and Ella June Miller pause for a moment of prayer*

before Sunday lunch, which has become a long-standing

tradition for the two of them. Eldon has served as pastor of the

Buckhorn Creek Mennonite Church in Rowdy, Kentucky,

for the past thirty-nine years.

Photograph by Gibbs Frazeur

▲ A young girl spends a few minutes with her dad

as they root for her brother at a soccer game

in Dallas, Texas.

Photograph by Doug Milner

Jesus Has a Family

BY TIM STAFFORD

one of us would even know that Jesus Christ exists if we had not been told by members of his family. . . . Jesus is invisible to us, but through his family he makes himself known.

The practical implication is that one place to look for a knowledge of Jesus is church, where Christians gather. And that is precisely where most people do look. If someone on the street gets a religious urge, he is likely to express it and explore it by going to church. There he will learn the plain facts about Jesus. But will he meet Jesus personally? Is the church the place to go if you want not just to know about him but to know him directly?

Annie Dillard writes that the most striking aspect of church services is that no one breaks out laughing. She has a strong sense of God's transcendent splendor, and the shuffling mechanics of church services seem drastically without splendor. I sometimes feel the same discrepancy. Where, in the swirl of Sunday clothes, outmoded music, a program somewhere between Rotary and TV talk, a ritual involving symbolic portions of bread and wine, and conversation in the Fireside Room over coffee—where do we find Jesus? If this is his family, how am I to see him in them? How exactly am I to see him in the crumpled face of an old lady who cannot get over her shock that the church has hung banners? How do I hear him in the voice of a teenage kid who keeps whispering to his girlfriend while the pastor speaks? The family of Jesus is very earthy and ordinary, and I want to know a heavenly Jesus who is truly extraordinary. Practically speaking, how is it possible?

I suspect many people feel this question. They come to church not because they have a particular taste for organ music, but because they are looking for the reality of Jesus. Where will they find him? Underneath the coffeepot? Hidden in an Easter lily? In the sermon? Will someone's mouth open during fellowship hour and Jesus' voice pour out?

To answer honestly and helpfully, we need to think about how Jesus' true identity is tied up in his family.

Jesus has a family, and if we want to know him, we must know the people he has chosen to be with, the people he has formed and still is forming. If we want to love him, we must love them. They are his children, and if we want to be his, we must become one of them. In them we will not only see the kind of work that Jesus does, but sometimes, fleetingly, we will see Jesus himself.

The body of Christ, like most families, has many faults. It is far from what it ought to be. It remains, however, the only human offspring of Jesus' personality. Many influences shape Jesus' family, but they never eradicate its origin. Blood does tell.

When someone "commits his life to Christ," he often knows far more about Jesus' family than he knows about Jesus himself. If you ask him to describe Jesus, he probably can only say something very general like "loving" or "compassionate." If you ask him to describe the particular group of Christians he is joining, however, he can say much more. A new Christian will not, typically, proceed immediately in an intensive study of the Gospels or to long hours of prayer and meditation to know Jesus better. Most of us are attracted to something far more earthly: a particular church, a parachurch group like Campus Life or InterVarsity, a Bible study group, a loose association of people, or even a single person whom we admire. We solidify our commitment to Jesus through a commitment to Jesus' family, as we find it locally. These people help determine the style of our new life in Jesus; we generally buy the same Bible translation, adopt the same religious phrases, make the same ethical choices, even learn to punctuate our prayers with the same phrases. We associate Jesus with that group and that style. We learn about Jesus indirectly as well as directly, through participating in his family.

Only later, if at all, do we begin to distinguish the group we are converted in from Jesus himself. Only then does Jesus become a distinctive character in our lives, someone we can "take with us" when we move to a new place. For some, however, the group's spirit and the Holy Spirit always seem indistinguishable.

I used to think that this cultural entrapment showed a highly disreputable side of Christianity. I suppose my ideal Christian was one big brain, detached from anything likely to make him lose his objectivity. This person would decide to become a Christian without being influenced by others; he would choose Jesus because of his study of the great world religions and philosophies. His style would spring straight from the New Testament.

I have changed my mind, not just because few such philosopher-Christians exist, but because I have seen that lonely, brainy Christians are not the most faithful to Jesus. They are often as adrift and disoriented as the freed slaves . . . : They have nowhere to call home. They tend to stay unhappy and unproductive, always learning but never knowing. By contrast, those who quickly become participants in Jesus' family grow in faith. We can forgive a great deal of cultural entrapment when we see active, fruitful lives. The reason for this vitality is obvious, if we think about faith as a personal relationship to Jesus. His flesh and blood carry more of his personality than a set of bloodless ideas. If we know Jesus' family, we are not far from knowing Jesus as a person rather than an idea.

After a morning worship service, the children look forward to a Fellowship time lunch at the Chinese Gospel Church in Southborough, Massachusetts.

Photograph by Jerry Valente

Not all who pray a prayer of commitment continue in faith. Those who do are usually, studies show, the ones who already have Christian friends or who very quickly make them. The others, whom we never see again, are not necessarily insincere; they just have no focal point for their prayers or decisions. Jesus is an abstraction and continues to be one because they do not know his visible family. This is why pioneer missionaries put as much of their energy into founding churches as they do into preaching the gospel. They know from hard experience that thousands of people may accept the Good News, but if they never form a family, the Good News will slowly dry up in their lives. Individual, atomistic Christians have no strength to endure. They almost never pass their faith on to others, even their own children. They need the nurturing of a Christian family.

So when a new Christian slavishly adopts the opinions and styles of a group of Christians he was converted in, we may have more cause for rejoicing than alarm. He will inevitably absorb cultural trappings that have very little to do with Jesus, but with them he will absorb the fundamental point of origin for the group: the life and love of Jesus. . . .

We have been asking where in our lives we can locate a personal relationship with Jesus. Yet Jesus has already touched us very personally through the Christians who brought us into his family. We have absorbed their style, their priorities, their personality—and through them, we have absorbed some of him. This does not end in our first year of new life; it goes on. He is the living source of our church family and our life. He shines through us, if darkly, and thus we become instruments of love toward one another.

Practically, what does this require of us? First, a deepening knowledge of Jesus involves a stubborn appreciation of the particular part of his family we were born into.

For example, I will always be a twentieth-century evangelical Protestant from a mainline denomination in America. Even if I react against that, it forms my reference point for understanding Jesus. Recognizing, even rebelling against, the limitations of our own spiritual background is a natural part of growing up. But real maturity comes when we accept those limitations and see beyond them to the fundamental character of Jesus. We must determine to see more than tired institutions in our native church; we must look for Jesus. A person who has never forgiven his parents for their failings can never be fully at peace with himself. Similarly, a Christian can never be entirely happy in his relationship to Jesus until he has come to peaceful, grateful terms with his spiritual family and can see in them part of the nature of Jesus. This perspective does not come cheaply; it may cost great conflict and inner turmoil.

▲ *The people of Pig River German Baptist Church in Franklin County, Virginia, value getting to know one another, visiting and eating together, and helping one another. Once a person decides to come into the German Baptist Church, they are required to follow a dress code that instills a sense of modesty and equity.*

Photograph by Andres R. Alonso

Second, a deepening knowledge of Jesus' family involves learning to know his family scattered in many strange places. . . . This widening consciousness of Jesus' family means becoming a world Christian, not bound by national or cultural borders. It also means becoming a historical Christian, recognizing that Jesus' family is not composed simply of those who happen to be walking around. We have the good fortune to follow on the experience of two thousand years of Christianity, twenty centuries of people expressing Jesus' nature in their various mental and physical circumstances. Not all the great men and women of God lived in the Bible period. Recognizing and appreciating the believers of the past is not merely an interesting piece of historic study; it is a way to see Jesus more clearly. His family is composed of all those who love and follow him, present and past. They are not dead! They live and love Jesus today! We are going to meet them and share a city with them.

Actually, we know them better than we realize. In our religious traditions, whether they are the ancient ones like the Catholic Mass or more recent ones like the altar call, we embody wisdom from our forefathers. Every Christian has a tradition; every local congregation does things the way they do not simply because the Bible says so but because their tradition has taught them that Jesus honors such procedures.

"We've always done it this way" need not be a curse. We do not have to accept tradition wholesale, but we ought not to scorn it wholesale either. Why, otherwise, have church buildings, choirs, Bible studies on Wednesday evenings? Why dress up for church? Why close our eyes and bow our heads to pray? Why have a missions committee? Why a Sunday school? Why a cross in the church? If we are determined to do without tradition—that is, to do without the witness of Christians who lived before us—we have to rethink everything. In the end, of course, we will only create a new set of human traditions.

Tradition is a link to the family of Jesus who lived before us. In it, we may find the imprint of Jesus. ‡

‡ *From Knowing the Face of God by Tim Stafford*

In 1915, when the founders of Madison Street Church first met in a rented store building in Oak Park, Illinois, they could not have foreseen the changes and growth ahead for their tiny church. Dr. Billy Graham was the guest speaker when the renamed Calvary Memorial Chapel moved to its present home in 1979, and today, well over a thousand people of diverse denominational backgrounds, including Kirk and Rattana Ito, worship together weekly at Calvary.

Photograph by Lee Balgemann

▲ Reverend Nicholas Katinas joins two parishioners in

marriage at the Holy Trinity Greek Orthodox Church on an

April Sunday afternoon in Dallas, Texas.

The bride and groom are adorned in the traditional wedding

"stephana," wreaths exchanged during the ceremony.

Photograph by Paula Nelson

The youngest generation looks on as the two newest ▲

additions to the Finn family are christened in

Father Flanagan's Boys Town Catholic Chapel

in Omaha, Nebraska.

Photograph by Rick Harrig

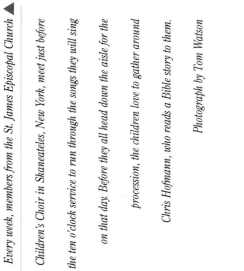

Every week, members from the St. James Episcopal Church

Children's Choir in Skaneateles, New York, meet just before

the ten o'clock service to run through the songs they will sing

on that day. Before they all head down the aisle for the

procession, the children love to gather around

Chris Hofmann, who reads a Bible story to them.

Photograph by Tom Watson

When he's not leading worship, professional musician

Dennis Jernigan can't think of anything more special than

spending time with his own family. Dennis, his wife,

Melinda, and their nine children live

on a farm in Boyton, Texas.

Photograph by Doug Hopfer

▲ *The congregation of St. Vincent de Paul Catholic Church*

in Nashville, Tennessee, join hands during Mass, signifying

the unity shared in Christ.

Photograph by Randy Piland

Commencement speaker Billy Graham congratulates his grandson, William Franklin Graham IV, during commencement exercises at Liberty University in Lynchburg, Virginia.

Photograph by Ron Londen

▲ Cuban Catholic parishioners hold an altar honoring

Our Lady of Charity and walk through the surrounding

neighborhood prior to entering church on Sunday morning.

Nearly twenty different nationalities are represented

by the Church of the Blessed Sacrament in the Mission

Hills/Jamaica Plain section of Boston, Massachusetts, led

by Father Michael McLellan, a Spanish-speaking Irish

American priest. Blessed Sacrament has more than 800

parishioners pass through its door on a Sunday morning.

Photograph by Dorothy Littell Greco

▲ "Blessing the Beasts"—Church members wait with their pets

just before the blessing of the animals, an old English

tradition, at St. James Episcopal Church

in Milton-Freewater, Oregon.

Photograph by Greg Lehman

Getting to Hope

BY KATHLEEN NORRIS

To get to Hope, turn south off U.S. Highway 12 at Keldron, South Dakota. It's easy to miss, as the town is not much more than a gas station and general store with a well-kept house behind it and a sign announcing that Cammy Varland of Keldron was Miss Teen South Dakota of 1987. . . . "Hope Presbyterian Church is located by itself on the South Dakota prairie" is what the church history says. But that doesn't begin to tell it. Hope Church, which fifteen years ago had a membership of forty-six, is down to twenty-five today, scattered on ranches for thirty miles around. The loss is due to older farmers retiring and moving to town and younger farmers leaving the area.

Hope Church is an unassuming frame building that stands in a pasture at the edge of a coulee where ash trees and berry bushes flourish; chokecherry, snowberry, buffalo berry. The place doesn't look like much, even when most of the membership has arrived on Sunday morning, yet it's one of the most successful churches I know. Along with Center School, the one-room schoolhouse that currently serves nine children from Grand Valley, Riverside, and Rolling Green townships in southwest Corson County, Hope Church gives the people who live around it a sense of identity.

"It doesn't matter what religion they are," says one longtime member. "The Lutherans and Catholics tell us that Hope is important to them, too, and becoming more so. We're *the church* in the neighborhood." A former pastor said of Hope Church, "It seemed that whatever was going on, a farm sale or a funeral or wedding, Hope was a part of what happened in that community." A measure of this may be seen at the annual Vacation Bible School for children, which is attended by both Lutheran and Catholic children. . . .

Hope is well-cared for. Both the outhouse and sanctuary are freshly painted. Two small, attractive stained-glass windows depicting a cross in the center of a sunburst and a dove with an olive branch flying over a landscape that resembles the fields around Hope Church were recently added to the south wall behind the pulpit, placed on either side of a handmade cross of varnished wood. The elegantly curved oak pews with carved endpieces are hand-me-downs from a church in Minnesota. A member of Hope drove his grain truck more than three hundred miles to get them.

Hope has a noble and well-used upright piano whose sound reminds me of the honky-tonk pianos in Western movies. But when Carolyn plays her quiet-down music at the beginning of a service, "Shall We Gather at the River" or "Holy, Holy, Holy," she's as effective as a Russian Orthodox deacon striding sternly through a service with censer and bells. We know it's time now to listen, that we will soon take our journey into word and song, and maybe change a little along the way. By the time we're into our first hymn, we know where we are. To paraphrase Isaiah 62, it's a place no longer desolate but delightful.

There is no indoor plumbing at Hope, but the congregation celebrates with food and drink at every opportunity. Once, when I arrived on Sunday, I noticed several popcorn poppers in a back pew. That was for after church, to help everyone get through the annual congregational meeting. . . .

In the manner of other tiny country churches I know . . . Hope is such a hospitable place that I suspect that no matter who you are or where you come from, you will be made to feel at home. But don't get so comfortable that you underestimate the people around you; don't entertain for a moment the notion that these farmers and ranchers are quaint country folk. Most of them have college degrees, though the figure is down slightly from 85 percent in the mid-1980s, a statistic that startled the pastor, who had last worked in Scranton, Pennsylvania, where 3 percent of her congregation was college educated.

Hope's people read, and they think about what is going on in the world. If you want to know anything about agriculture on a global scale—the cattle market in Argentina or prospects for the wheat crop in Australia—this is the place to ask. As one pastor recently put it, "the thing that makes Hope so vibrant is that the congregation is so alive to the world."

Hope's members take seriously their responsibility as members of the world's diverse and largely poor human race. A few years ago, reasoning that people who raise food (and often have a hard time getting a price for it that covers their expenses) should know more about why so many in the world can't afford to feed themselves, they conducted a study on the politics of hunger. To conclude the study, they invited an expert on the subject to come from Chicago to address churchpeople in the area. They also studied the ethical issues of raising animals for food. As farmers who know the life history and temperament of every cow in their herds, they were dismayed to discover the inroads factory farming is making in American agriculture.

In recent hard times, while Hope's membership declined by nearly half, the amount the church donates for missions has increased every year. It now ranks near the top in per capita giving among Presbyterian churches in the state of South Dakota.

Beech Creek Wesleyan, in Beech Creek, Pennsylvania, prides itself on its family friendly atmosphere.

Photograph by Bob Hagle

One former pastor said, "It can be astonishing how tiny Hope Church makes you feel so strongly that you're part of a global entity." . . . For this and other reasons pastors find the Hope congregation stimulating to work with. One told me if he could sum them up in one word, it would be "appreciative." Another said: "Hope is where I realized how much the members of a rural church actually work as well as worship together. They live supporting each other. We'd spoken of such things at seminary as an ideal, but this was the first time in twenty years of ministry I'd actually seen it done. It made me realize how vital a small country church can be."

Perhaps it's not surprising that so tiny a rural congregation is not often well served by the larger church of which it is a part. For all their pious talk of "small is beautiful," church bureaucrats, like bureaucrats everywhere, concentrate their attention on places with better demographics; bigger numbers, more power and money. The power of Hope Church and country churches like it is subtle and not easily quantifiable. It's a power derived from smallness and lack of power, a concept the apostle Paul would appreciate, even if modern church bureaucrats lose sight of it. . . .

I find it ironic that the new inclusiveness of the official church tends to exclude people as rural as those of Hope. But I may have been spoiled by the company I keep on the prairie, the Benedictine monks and country people, some well-educated, some not, who know from their experience that prayer is important, that worship serves a purpose, that God is part of everyday life, and that singing "Nearer My God, to Thee" may be good for a person. It's a rural hymn: It's the rare city person who can imagine sleeping out in the open, a stone for a pillow and a heaven of stars above. . . .

And yet I wonder. I wonder if a church like Hope doesn't teach the world in the way a monastery does, not by loudly voicing its views but by existing quietly in its own place. . . . Monks, with their conscious attempt to do the little things peaceably and well—daily things like liturgy or chores, or preparing and serving meals—have a lot in common with the farmers and ranchers of Hope.

Hope Church, south of Keldron, is a real place, a holy place; you know that when you first see it, one small building in a vast land. You know it when you walk in the door. It can't be moved from where it is on the prairie. Physically, yes, but that's beside the point. Hope's people are traditional people, country people, and they know that the spirits of a place cannot be transported or replaced. They're second-, third-, fourth-generation Americans who have lived on the land for many years, apart from the mainstream of American culture, which has become more urban with every passing year. Hope's people have become one with their

Services at the Old Sheldon Church in Beaufort, South Carolina, are reminiscent of a "Great Gatsby" lawn party. It's not unusual to see men in suits with bow ties and women in flower-print dresses wearing big floppy hats. Held the second Sunday following Easter, the service is a time for celebration of spring and God's promise of renewal.

Photograph by Rick Harrig

place: this is not romanticism, but truth. . . .

Hope is small, dying, and beautifully alive. It's tribal in a way, as most of its members are related. But it does not suffer from tribalism, the deadening and often deadly insularity that can cause groups of people to fear or despise anyone who is not like them. I find in Hope many of the graces of a monastery with stability of place and a surprisingly wide generosity in its hospitality . . . .

The people of Hope live far apart from each other on the land: Paradoxically, I suspect this is one reason they seem better at creating community than people in town, better at being together while leaving each other alone, as I once heard the monastic ideal defined . . . .

It's absurd, too, that I find a Benedictine monastery and a tiny Presbyterian church in the middle of nowhere to be so absolutely and perfectly complementary. I am not showing due respect to religion as I was taught it . . . But then, I don't have to. This is the Wild West. Out at Hope, in the summer, bellowing cows at a nearby watering tank sometimes join in the call to worship; one year, baby rattlesnakes showed up for Vacation Bible School. . . .

One former minister at Hope who had come from the urban East told me . . . she couldn't imagine what was happening at the first funeral service she conducted for a member of Hope Church when, as people gathered for the graveside service, the men, some kneeling, began studying the open grave. It was early November, and someone explained that they were checking the frost and moisture levels in the ground. They were farmers and ranchers worried about a drought. They were mourners giving a good friend back to the earth. They were people of the earth, looking for a sign of hope. ‡

‡ *From Dakota: A Spiritual Geography by Kathleen Norris*

Sher Emerick-Cayton and Diana Lyster prepare for a Mother's

Day buffet in Canoles Hall following services at the

First Presbyterian Church of San Rafael in California.

Photograph by Dave Bartruff

▶ A Sunday worship service is conducted by Motor Racing
Outreach prior to the NASCAR Winston Cup race at
Martinsville Speedway in Virginia. Motor Racing Outreach
was founded in 1988 by Max Helton to minister
to the Winston Cup community.

▲ Former Winston Cup champion Darrell Waltrip
with his wife, Stevie, and their daughter, Sarah Kaitlyn,
enjoy participating in the Motor Racing Outreach services.

Photographs by Andres R. Alonso

Youth gather for morning devotions at the ▲
North Texas Methodist Youth Camp
in Bridgeport, Texas.

Photograph by Louis DeLuca

Sharing Hearts

IN SERVICE

From Bibles to bumper stickers. From books to cassettes. From sermons to smidgens of advice. All of them come full of words. Good words, many of them. Well-intentioned words, certainly. But words that have not been made flesh. Words that have not dwelt among us.

I wonder what would happen if one day all of those words went away.

What if one day the entire body of Christ were struck dumb? Couldn't write a word. Couldn't speak a word. Couldn't even move our lips to mouth one. What then? What would be left?

Our lives.

And what would our lives say? What would they say about who we are and who our God is? What would they say about what we believe? If we were to take away the words, how much of the gospel could the world understand?

Would we discover that the world is illiterate? Or that our lives are illegible?

Would the writing on the pages of our lives, which we

▲ *During "Christmas in April" volunteers in Hartsville,*
South Carolina, work in impoverished areas,
painting, repairing, and remodeling homes. Roofs
are replaced, siding and porches painted, walls
and floors reinforced, and all labor and
materials are donated free-of-charge to the
homeowners.

Photograph by Rob Nelson

always took to be literature, turn out to be the scribbling of a preschooler? Or would the pages simply be blank?

"Preach the gospel," Saint Francis said, "and when necessary, use words." And he said that, I think, because he realized that the most impactful words are those incarnate in our lives. Words that have been made flesh and dwell among us.

When asked why he wanted to go to Africa to work among the natives, Albert Schweitzer said it was because he wanted his life to be his sermon. He wanted the days of his week to be a Sunday text so clear and so compelling that little else needed to be said. As it turned out, little else needed be. His life was heard by millions.

There is a story of another missionary whose life was not heard by millions. He was an English missionary in India whose mission board required him to keep detailed financial records for which he had to be skilled at double-entry bookkeeping. Which he wasn't. He had no background in accounting or business. He only had a calling. To be a missionary. But his balances were always off, and the separate accounts he was supposed to keep kept getting mixed, and so the

mission board released him. Unfit for the mission field, was their assessment, when in truth, he was only unfit for book-keeping. He left without incident. Nobody knew where.

Years later, a woman missionary visited a remote jungle village to introduce the natives to Jesus. She told them of His kindness and His love for the poor, how He went to their homes to eat with them, how He visited them when they were sick, how He fed the hungry, healed the sick, bound up the wounds of the brokenhearted, and how children loved to follow Him.

The eyes of the natives lit up, their faces beamed, and one of them exclaimed:

"Miss Sahib, we know him well; he has been living here for years!"

When they took her to see him, it was the man who years earlier had been dismissed by the mission board. He had settled there to do his work, sequestered from the double-entried tyranny of bookkeeping. Whenever anyone was sick, he visited them and waited up all night outside their hut if necessary, checking on them, tending to their needs. When they were hurt, he nursed their wounds. For the old and the infirm, he brought food and water. When cholera broke out in the village, he went from hut to hut, doing what he could to help.

I wonder. If someone were to come to our village, our neighborhood, our place of work, and that person began to describe Jesus, would anybody hearing the description say, "We know Him well; He has been living here for years!" ‡

Haroutun Mulian, who at ninety-seven years of age

is the oldest member of the local Armenian community,

greets one of the youngest, four-month-old George Avetikyan,

at a Sunday afternoon picnic at Johnson Park

in Grand Rapids, Michigan.

Photograph by Wende Alexander Clark

▲ Henry Gehrke tenderly kisses his wife, Frieda, one Sunday

morning at their home in Ridgefield, Washington.

Henry and Frieda were married in 1933 and have three

children and over sixty grand- and great-grandchildren.

Grandma Frieda, who has lost her sight and her ability to

walk, is looking forward to seeing the Lord soon and dancing

with joy with her "resurrection legs."

Photograph by Louis Bencze

Wil Story, on behalf of the Sunday School, ▲

presents flowers to his grandfather, Pastor Ken Story,

during a morning service as the Germantown

Baptist Church in Germantown, Tennessee,

celebrates the retirement of their pastor

after thirty-two years of service.

Photograph by Karim Shamsi-Basha

▲ *Youth group members of the Immanuel Presbyterian Church*

of Warrenville, Illinois, work alongside prisoners from a

nearby minimum-security prison to fill and lay sandbags

during devastating midwestern floods.

Photograph by William Koechling

Boys from Our Lady of Mount Carmel Roman Catholic ▲

Church in Brooklyn, New York, work together to lift a replica

of the Giglio tower in celebration of the Feast of Saint

Paulinus. For over one hundred years, men at Our Lady of

Mount Carmel Church have participated in the Giglio

Festival tradition of carrying a tower weighing over 5,000

pounds through the streets of the city, as done in Naples,

Italy. For many young men, this feat of strength

becomes an initiation into adulthood.

Photograph by Ethel Wolvovitz

▲ Lt. Glen Doss, an officer of the Salvation Army, counsels a local

resident of Canoga Park, California. The Salvation Army may be

best known for its bell ringers during the Christmas season, but

the organization makes a difference year-round through its

community centers, rehabilitation programs, food and shelter for

the homeless programs, social services, support to families

involved with correctional facilities, and emergency and disaster

relief, as well as thrift stores and other volunteer services in local

communities. The Salvation Army is one of the most respected

ministries in America and throughout the world.

Photograph by Tara C. Patty

Catie Conner, dancing a traditional Davidic ▲

dance, is a part of Baruch Ha Shem, a Christian

Messianic community that expresses the Jewishness

of Biblical faith through Torah reading, observance

of Biblical feast days, teaching of scripture from

a Jewish perspective, Messianic praise

music, and Davidic dance.

Photograph by Doug Hopfer

▲ Volunteer Andy Sanchez loads emergency food to

be delivered by New Mexico social worker Severo

Sisneros through the services of the Storehouse.

This Albuquerque-based ministry to

the homeless and working poor was begun in 1970

to carry out works of mercy. Some 150 volunteers

from over sixty area churches joined last year to

serve 45,000 free meals, distribute 36,000

bags of clothing, and to repair and distribute

household items.

Photograph by Jonathan A. Meyers

A volunteer repairs a baby carriage in a workshop of ▲

the Storehouse. The Storehouse manages to provide

over $1.5 million worth of goods and services on an

annual budget of less than $165,000.

Photograph by Jonathan A. Meyers

Stars and Servants

BY PHILIP YANCEY

My career as a journalist has afforded me opportunities to interview diverse people. Looking back, I can roughly divide them into two types: stars and servants. The stars include NFL football greats, movie actors, music performers, famous authors, TV personalities, and the like. These are the people who dominate our magazines and our television programs. We fawn over them, poring over the minutiae of their lives: the clothes they wear, the food they eat, the aerobic routines they follow, the people they love, the toothpaste they use.

Yet I must tell you that, in my limited experience, these our "idols" are as miserable a group of people as I have ever met. Most have troubled or broken marriages. Nearly all are hopelessly dependent on psychotherapy. In a heavy irony, these larger-than-life heroes seem tormented by incurable self-doubt.

I have also spent time with servants. People like Dr. Paul Brand, who worked for twenty years among outcasts—the poorest of the poor, leprosy patients in rural India. Or the health workers who left high-paying jobs to serve with Mendenhall Ministries in a backwater town of Mississippi. Or relief workers in Somalia, Sudan, Ethiopia, Bangladesh, or other such repositories of world-class human suffering. Or the Ph.D.'s scattered throughout jungles of South America translating the Bible into obscure languages.

I was prepared to honor and admire these servants, to hold them up as inspiring examples. I was not, however, prepared to envy them. But as I now reflect on the two groups side by side, stars and servants, the servants clearly emerge as the favored ones, the graced ones. They work for low pay, long hours, and no applause, "wasting" their talents and skills among the poor and uneducated. But somehow in the process of losing their lives they have found them. They have received the "peace that is not of this world."

* * *

I first met Bill Leslie in a grungy pizza parlor after a DePaul University basketball game. I was surprised to find an overweight white man who dressed carelessly, talked too loud, and laughed uproariously at his own jokes. This was the minister of

Chicago's renowned LaSalle Street Church?

Out of curiosity I attended LaSalle the following Sunday, and ended up staying there for thirteen years. I got to know Bill well, especially after my wife accepted a job directing one of the church's outreach programs. Bill talked too loud in the pulpit, too, laughed at his own oft-repeated jokes, and occasionally slaughtered the English language. But he became our pastor, and we grew to love him, and when he died unexpectedly of a heart attack at the age of sixty, Janet and I joined many other Chicagoans in grieving the loss.

Bill Leslie served the same church for twenty-eight years, and what a time it was. The congregation met in a building whose walls can tell the history of Chicago: German-speaking Lutherans laid the cornerstone in 1882, and Italians, Japanese, and Appalachian whites all took turns in the building until hippies and then yuppies moved in. When Bill became pastor in 1961, the church stood midway between the richest and poorest communities in Chicago. Two blocks to the east lay the Gold Coast, average income over $50,000; two blocks to the west lay the Cabrini-Green housing project, average income under $3,000.

While studying the biblical prophets' words on justice, LaSalle caught a vision of being a "bridge church" between the two neighborhoods.

After several years of commuting from the comfortable suburb of Wheaton, Bill Leslie heard God's call to join the neighborhood. It was 1968, the worst time possible for such a move. After Martin Luther King, Jr.'s assassination, angry blacks burned down thirty square blocks of buildings; the church stuck out amid the rubble, preserved because of its good reputation in the community. National Guardsmen patrolled the streets. The Leslies could find no one willing to insure their urban home.

A few years later, three men attacked Bill in the sanctuary, hoping to steal the morning offering. They hit him on the head with a bowling pin, stomped on his groin, and battered him with a fire extinguisher. Stripped of clothing, gagged, hogtied, Bill lay in the vestibule and reconsidered his call to the city.

But he did not give up. Too much was happening in the fledgling congregation for him to walk away. Neighborhood outreach started when Sunday school teachers, noticing that many students could not read, offered tutoring classes after the Sunday service. The need was enormous—the local high school had a dropout rate of 75 percent. Soon busloads of students from nearby evangelical Wheaton College were making their way to LaSalle Street to help with one-on-one tutoring. Since unemployment among the working-age population of Cabrini averaged 86 percent, most kids from the projects

The Highway and Hedges Outreach Ministry is a nondenominational ministry in Milwaukee, Wisconsin, that serves gang members, the sick, poor, addicted, abused, and imprisoned.

Photograph by John J. Kovom

hung out on street corners all day. During summer months, someone in the neighborhood is shot an average of once every other day. Bill and others at the church saw a need for recreational programs. They bought a pool table, set up a basketball court, and raised money for football equipment (the high school team, with only thirteen helmets, was scrimmaging with seven players lined up on offense and six on defense). Before long, an urban Young Life program had sprung up, affiliated with the church.

More needs surfaced. When a government study reported that a third of all dog and cat food was bought by senior citizens too poor to afford "people food," the church began a ministry to local seniors. To counter neighborhood abuse by the police and by landlords, an attorney quit his firm to begin a Legal Aid Clinic, offering free legal representation to any Cabrini-Green resident with qualifying income. A counseling center was established, with sliding fees based on income.

In Chicago, as in most cities, half of all babies are born to single mothers, and soon the church founded a ministry to assist them as well. Bill was most proud, however, of a housing project that he first dreamed of when the church's annual budget was $20,000. Somehow, with LaSalle leading the way to secure grants and loans, the $11 million development became a reality. Economically and racially mixed, Atrium Village is credited with anchoring the community and reversing neighborhood decay. . . . .

Bill did some things wrong, but he got one thing right: He understood the grace of God. Grace became the church's theme: Its fifty-year anniversary banquet featured a large banner that read, "This far by grace."

Bill recognized his own endless need for grace, preached it almost every Sunday, and offered it to everyone around him in starkly practical ways. Because of his faithfulness, the near-north side of Chicago is a different place today. And so, I believe, is heaven. ‡

▲ *Women of Lighthouse Church of Christ and God in Watts, California, lead the singing during a Christmas service titled, "Streets of Gold."*

Photograph by Mark Richards

‡ *From* I Was Just Wondering *and* Finding God in Unexpected Places *by Philip Yancey*

▶ Carl Knight and his wife, JoAnn, run the San Francisco

Gospel Mission, in San Francisco, California, which is open

every day of the year. Carl, Superintendent

since 1981, has been associated with the mission for over

forty-five years. JoAnn joined him in his work there in 1962

when they married. The mission holds worship

services nightly, and Carl preaches every Sunday morning.

Photograph by Craig Lee

115

▲ A member of the Salvation Army trumpets the Good

News on Easter Sunday at Portsmith Square in

Chinatown, San Francisco, California.

Photograph by Gary Fong

Team Chaplin Jimmy Chalmers talks with the players ▲

of the Durham Bulls, a class A affiliate of the Atlanta Braves,

in the team's indoor batting cage during what they call

"baseball chapel," just prior to a Sunday home game.

Photograph by Walt Unks

Former President Jimmy Carter looks on as Chelsea

Clinton gets a hammering lesson during a Habitat for

Humanity work day in Atlanta, Georgia. Habitat for

Humanity International, begun by Millard Fuller in 1987,

builds new homes for the needy throughout the world with

the help of volunteer muscle and donated materials. New

homeowners are required to donate 500 hours of labor

themselves on the new home. Above, Chelsea and President

Clinton join former President Jimmy Carter and others,

including new homeowner Mattie Jackson, in a moment of

prayer during the Atlanta work day.

Photographs by Rob Nelson

New Rags for Old

BY WALTER WANGERIN, JR.

I saw a strange sight. I stumbled upon a story most strange, like nothing my life, my street sense, my sly tongue had ever prepared me for.

Hush child. Hush, now, and I will tell it to you.

Even before dawn one Friday morning I noticed a young man, handsome and strong, walking the alleys of our City. He was pulling an old cart filled with clothes both bright and new, and he was calling in a clear, tenor voice: "Rags!" Ah, the air was foul and the first light filthy to be crossed by such sweet music.

"Rags! New rags for old! I take your tired rags! Rags!"

"Now, this is a wonder," I thought to myself, for the man stood six-feet-four, and his arms were like tree limbs, hard and muscular, and his eyes flashed intelligence. Could he find no better job than this, to be a ragman in the inner city?

I followed him. My curiosity drove me. And I wasn't disappointed.

Soon the Ragman saw a woman sitting on her back porch. She was sobbing into a handkerchief, sighing and shedding a thousand tears. Her knees and elbows made a sad X. Her shoulders shook. Her heart was breaking.

The Ragman stopped his cart. Quietly, he walked to the woman, stepping round tin cans, dead toys, and Pampers.

"Give me your rag," he said so gently, "and I'll give you another."

He slipped the handkerchief from her eyes. She looked up, and he laid across her palm a linen cloth so clean and new that it shined. She blinked from the gift to the giver.

Then, as he began to pull his cart again, the Ragman did a strange thing: He put her stained handkerchief to his own face; and then *he* began to weep, to sob as grievously as she had done, his shoulders shaking. Yet she was left without a tear.

"This *is* a wonder," I breathed to myself, and I followed the sobbing Ragman like a child who cannot turn away from mystery.

"Rags! Rags! New rags for old!"

In a little while, when the sky showed gray behind the rooftops and I could see the shredded curtains hanging out black windows, the Ragman came upon a girl whose head was wrapped in a bandage, whose eyes were empty. Blood soaked her bandage. A single line of blood ran down her cheek.

Now the tall Ragman looked upon this child with pity, and he drew a lovely yellow bonnet from his cart.

"Give me your rag," he said, tracing his own line on her cheek, "and I'll give you mine."

The child gazed at him while he loosened the bandage, removed it, and tied it to his own head. The bonnet he set on hers. And I gasped at what I saw: for with the bandage went the wound! Against his brow it ran a darker, more substantial blood—his own!

"Rags! Rags! I take old rags!" cried the sobbing, bleeding, strong, intelligent Ragman.

The sun hurt both the sky, now, and my eyes; the Ragman seemed more and more to hurry.

"Are you going to work?" he asked a man who leaned against a telephone pole.

The man shook his head.

The Ragman pressed him: "Do you need a job?"

"Are you crazy?" sneered the other. He pulled away from the pole, revealing the right sleeve of his jacket—flat, the cuff stuffed into the pocket. He had no arm.

"So," said the Ragman. "Give me your jacket, and I'll give you mine."

Such quiet authority in his voice!

The one-armed man took off his jacket. So did the Ragman—and I trembled at what I saw: for the Ragman's arm stayed in its sleeve, and when the other put it on he had two good arms, thick as tree limbs; but the Ragman had only one.

"Go to work," he said.

After that he found a drunk, lying unconscious beneath an army blanket, an old man, hunched, wizened, and sick. He took that blanket and wrapped it round himself, but for the drunk he left new clothes.

And now I had to run to keep up with the Ragman. Though he was weeping uncontrollably and bleeding freely at the forehead, pulling his cart with one arm, stumbling for drunkenness, falling again and again, exhausted, old, old and sick, yet he went with terrible speed. On spider's legs he skittered through the alleys of the City, this mile and the next, until he came to its limits, and then he rushed beyond.

I wept to see the change in this man. I hurt to see his sorrow. And yet I needed to

The Lighthouse Church of Christ and God ▶ stands as a beacon among the urban people in Los Angeles, California. On this cold December night, children from a homeless family found shelter and warmth when Lighthouse opened its facilities to them.

Photograph by Mark Richards

see where he was going in such haste, perhaps to know what drove him so.

The little old Ragman—he came to a landfill. He came to the garbage pits. And then I wanted to help him in what he did, but I hung back, hiding. He climbed a hill. With tormented labor he cleared a little space on that hill. Then he sighed. He lay down. He pillowed his head on a handkerchief and a jacket. He covered his bones with an army blanket. And he died.

Oh, how I cried to witness that death! I slumped in a junked car and wailed and mourned as one who has no hope—because I had come to love the Ragman. Every other face had faded in the wonder of this man, and I cherished him; but he died. I sobbed myself to sleep.

I did not know—how could I know?—that I slept through Friday night and Saturday and its night, too.

But then, on Sunday morning, I was wakened by a violence.

Light—pure, hard, demanding light—slammed against my sour face, and I blinked, and I looked, and I saw the last and the first wonder of all. There was the Ragman, folding the blanket most carefully, a scar on his forehead, but alive! And, besides that, healthy! There was no sign of sorrow nor of age, and all the rags that he had gathered shined for cleanliness.

Well, then I lowered my head, and trembling for all that I had seen, I myself walked up to the Ragman. I told him my name with shame, for I was a sorry figure next to him. Then I took off all my clothes in that place, and I said to him with dear yearning in my voice: "Dress me."

He dressed me. My Lord, he put new rags on me, and I am a wonder beside him. The Ragman, the Ragman, the Christ! ‡

▲ *Clinton Beckenridge, a former gang member, finds being*

a part of the community at Lighthouse Church of Christ

and God helpful in getting his feet back on the ground.

One of the greatest joys in his day is visiting with

neighbors and sharing about his faith.

Photograph by Mark Richards

‡ *From* Ragman, and Other Cries of Faith *by Walter Wangerin, Jr.*

Sister Mary Catherine of the Brothers and Sisters of Charity ▶

of the Little Portion prepares the evening meal early on

a Sunday morning at the monastery in Grandrieu, Arkansas.

Sister Mary Catherine is assisted by her mother,

Jackie Breidt, who is visiting from New York.

Photograph by David Bell

BY KEN GIRE

Growing Strong
IN SPIRIT

I used to put people who talked about God speaking to them in dreams in the same category as palm readers . . . until that person was my wife.

The dream she had was set in a huge gymnasium. Windows lined the top of the thirty-foot walls, letting in diffused rays of sunlight. She was sitting on the floor with a young man she didn't recognize but somehow felt she knew. The two of them were watching a ballet where hundreds of beautiful dancers in soft gowns were dancing. It was the most wonderful dance she had ever seen. Though her body wasn't moving, everything inside her was caught up in the dance and she felt part of it, one with it, and it filled her senses so fully she felt she would never tire of it.

The young man stood up and walked to the center of the gym. As he did, the ballerinas all bowed before him and floated on their toes to the far walls. Then he made an announcement: "Now I want *her* to dance."

A pastor prays with a couple in crisis.

Our families are strengthened through the prayers and practical support offered by our larger family of believers.

Photograph by Michael Lewis

Judy realized he was talking about her.

She got up and walked to where he was standing. Once by his side, she realized she was wearing grubby-looking workout clothes with torn leggings. But her concern was only momentary. When the young man left the center of the floor and sat down to watch, she began to dance. She swung her leg up high, turning her body in the opposite direction as she did, and then danced to the end of the gym. Each time she reached one end, she swung her foot high in the air, pivoted on the other foot, turned and danced to the other end.

Then, as quickly as she started dancing, she stopped and sat down beside the young man. He walked to the center of the gym and addressed the ballerinas: "See how beautifully she dances. She has had no training, yet see how she dances. I love her dance."

As little Judy left the gym floor, the ballerinas resumed their places, and the ballet continued. The young man took her aside and showed her a photo album filled with pictures of a beautiful house. The rooms were lavish and the furnishings exquisite. As she marveled over them, he said: "This is my home. I want you to make your home there and dance for me."

When Judy woke from the dream, she couldn't understand it. It was so vivid in her memory yet so vague in its meaning. She knew God had spoken in the past to people through dreams. Both Old and New Testaments were full of such accounts. But did

▲ *Sunday wrapped up a four-day*

crusade at Cooper Stadium in

Columbus, Ohio, where more than

50,000 people had a chance to

hear the gospel message spoken by

Reverend Billy Graham.

Photograph by James D. DeCamp

He still? She didn't know.

She got dressed and took the kids to school with little thought of the dream. After she finished her morning routine, though, she was driving home, and the dream came back to her. Vividly came back to her. As she was watching herself dance, her thoughts were interrupted by memories she had long since forgotten. Memories of when she was a young girl.

During her growing-up years when it was her turn to do dishes, Judy would dawdle at the sink. She would dip a dish into the soapy water, blow a bubble, think about something a minute, wash the dish, play with the water, think about something else, rinse the dish. And sometimes this would go on all evening until the dishes were done.

But when no one was around, young Judy would leave the dishes and dance back and forth from the kitchen to the living room. Each time she would come to the end of the room, she would swing one foot high in the air, pivot on the other foot, turn, and dance to the other end.

When that memory came back to her, a flood of tears came with it, tears for the little girl who carried so much sadness within her, never letting it come to the surface, never telling anyone her dreams or her heartaches.

Then suddenly it dawned on her.

The young man in the dream. It was Jesus. He had been there, watching her dance in that living room during those painful years of growing up. He knew her longings to be a ballerina. He knew she had no training. Knew she had to drop out of college to go to work. Knew the feelings of inadequacy she held so fragilely within her. Feelings that she was nobody special, that her life didn't matter, that other people could teach the Bible but not her, that good things happened to other people but not to her, that other people had interesting lives but not her.

Yet Jesus wanted *her*. Out of all the ballerinas, he picked *her* to dance for him, picked *her* to come to his house. It didn't make any difference that she didn't have any training or that she didn't have the lovely outfits the other ballerinas had. She had the heart of a ballerina. And she loved to dance. Those were the things that mattered.

Judy called me at work to tell me about the dream, not knowing how I would react but needing to tell me because it was such a beautiful dream and had touched her so deeply.

"So," I said, after she finished, "are you saying you want ballet lessons?"

"It's not about ballet," she said. "It's His way of telling me that He was there. Back then, when I was younger, He saw me. Nobody else saw me, but *He* saw me. I think, I don't know, but I think the dream was about His being pleased with me and about His delight in my worship of Him, and I think He's inviting me into a more intimate relationship with Him."

A young parishioner resting on the Word of God at Rose Hill Missionary Baptist Church in Jayless, Mississippi.

Photograph by Jame Edward Bates

Rich Reinert, a teacher during the school year and a pro rodeo clown during the summer circuit, pauses for a word of prayer before entering the ring at the Cody Stampede Rodeo in Cody, Wyoming.

Photograph by Dewey Vanderhoff

Joshua Jackson, Allison Ende, Emily Brown, Eduardo Mandujano, and Fidel Ovalle anxiously await their First Holy Communion at Holy Cross Catholic Church in Lansing, Michigan.

Photograph by Michael Schimpf

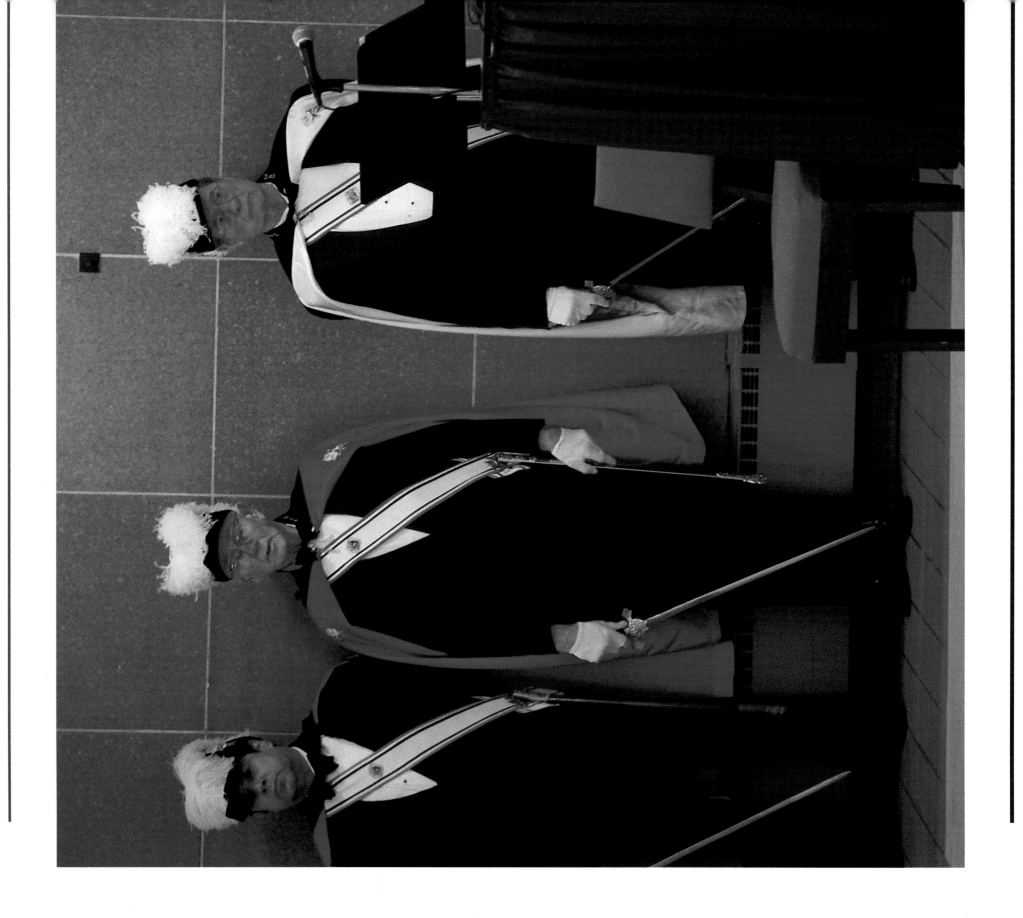

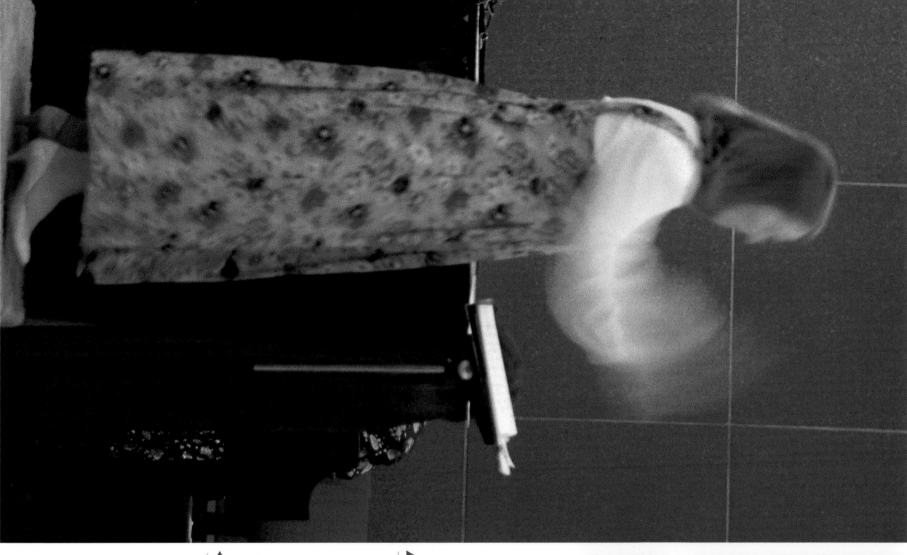

▶ "He is Risen!" proclaims Lisa King to the Calvary
Memorial Church audience, while portraying a woman
who witnesses Jesus Christ's resurrection from the tomb
during Easter Sunday drama in Oak Park, Illinois.

Photograph by Lee Balgemann

▲ Members of the Knights of Columbus stand guard as Carol
Finney directs the choir during a confirmation service at
Christ the King Catholic Church in Kansas City, Kansas.
The Knights of Columbus is a men's organization that
participates in formal functions and helps raise funds for
Catholic charities.

Photograph by Don Wolf

▲ *Grandparents Edina and Cecil Stevens take their grandson,*

Jason, whom they are raising, to church every Sunday.

Photograph by Paula Nelson

A Sunday school student in earnest prayer at the ▲

First Presbyterian Church in Chattanooga, Tennessee.

Photograph by David B. Jenkins

Good God

BY FREDERICK BUECHNER

Jesus made his Church out of human beings with more or less the same mixture in them of cowardice and guts, of intelligence and stupidity, of selfishness and generosity, of openness of heart and sheer cussedness as you would be apt to find in any of us. The reason he made his Church out of human beings is that human beings were all there was to make it out of. In fact as far as I know, human beings are all there is to make it out of still. It's a point worth remembering.

It is also a point worth remembering that even after Jesus made these human beings into a Church, they seem to have gone right on being human beings. They actually knew Jesus as their friend. They sat at his feet and listened to him speak; they ate with him and tramped the countryside with him; they witnessed his miracles; but not even all of that turned them into heroes. They kept on being as human as they'd always been with most of the same strengths and most of the same weaknesses.

And finally when it comes to remembering things, we do well to keep in mind that the idea of becoming the Church wasn't their idea. It was Jesus' idea. It was Jesus who made them a Church. They didn't come together the way like-minded people come together to make a club. They didn't come together the way a group of men might come together to form a baseball team or the way a group of women might come together to lobby for higher teachers' salaries. They came together because Jesus called them to come together. . . .

Somebody appears on your front stoop speaking your name, say, and you go down to open the door to see what's up. Sometimes while it's still raining, the sun comes out from behind the clouds, and suddenly, arching against the gray sky, there is a rainbow, which people stop doing whatever they're doing to look at. They lay down their fishing nets, their tax forms, their bridge hands, their golf clubs or newspapers, to gaze at the sky because what is happening up there is so marvelous they can't help themselves. Something like that, I think, is the way those twelve men Matthew names were called to become a church, plus Mary, Martha, Joanna, and all the other women and men who one way or another became a part of it too. One way or another Christ called them. That's how it happened. They saw the marvel of him arch across the grayness of things—the grayness of their own lives perhaps, of life itself. They heard his voice calling their names. And they went.

They seem to have gone right on working at pretty much whatever they'd been working at before, which means that he didn't so much call them out of their ordinary lives as he called them out of believing that ordinary life is ordinary. He called them to see that no matter how ordinary it may seem to us as we live it, life is extraordinary. "The Kingdom of God is at hand" is the way he put it to them, and the way he told them to put it to others. Life, even at its most monotonous and backbreaking and heart-numbing, has the Kingdom buried in it the way a field has treasure buried in it, he said. The Kingdom of God is as close to us as some precious keepsake we've been looking for for years, which is lying just in the next room under the rug all but crying out to us to come find it.

If we only had eyes to see and ears to hear and wits to understand, we would know that the Kingdom of God in the sense of holiness, goodness, beauty is as close as breathing and is crying out to be born both within ourselves and within the world; we would know that the Kingdom of God is what we all of us hunger for above all other things even when we don't know its name or realize that it's what we're starving to death for. The Kingdom of God is where our best dreams come from and our truest prayers. We glimpse it at those moments when we find ourselves being better than we are and wiser than we know. . . .

A fat man drives by in his Chevy pickup with a cigarette in his mouth and on his rear bumper a sticker that says *Jesus Loves You.* There's a shotgun slung across the back window. He is not a stranger we've never seen before and couldn't care less if we ever see again. He is our brother, our father. He is our son. It is true that we have never seen him before, and that we will probably never see him again—just that one quick glimpse as he goes by at twenty-five miles an hour because it is a school zone—but if we can somehow fully realize the truth of that, fully understand that this is the one and only time we will ever see him, we will treasure that one and only time the way we treasure the rainbow in the sky or the ring we finally found under the rug after years of looking for it. The old woman with thick glasses who sits in front of us at the movies eating popcorn is our mother, our sister, our child grown old, and once we know that, once we see her for who she truly is, everything about her becomes precious—the skinny back of her neck, the way she puts her hand over her mouth when she laughs.

These are not ordinary people any more than life is ordinary. They are extraordinary people. Life is extraordinary, and the extraordinariness of it is what Jesus calls the Kingdom of God. The extraordinariness of it is that in the Kingdom of

Gospel tunes set the pace for this churchgoer one Sunday morning on Blount Street in downtown Raleigh, North Carolina.

Photograph by Doug Van De Zande

God we all belong to each other the way families do. We are all of us brothers and sisters in it. We are all of us mothers and fathers and children of each other in it because that is what we are called together as the Church to be. That is what the Church means. We are called by God to love each other the way Jesus says that God has loved us. That is the Good News about God—the Gospel—which he came to proclaim. Loving each other and loving God is what the kingdom is. No scientific truth or philosophic truth, no truth of art or music or literature, is as important as that Kingdom truth. . . .

Our happiness is all mixed up with each other's happiness and our peace with each other's peace. Our own happiness, our own peace, can never be complete until we find some way of sharing it with people who the way things are now have no happiness and know no peace. . . .

The old woman has gone to the movies to help take her mind off the fact that she has cancer. Cancer is a sickness that you and I don't know how to heal, more's the pity, but it is not her only sickness. Her other sickness is being lonely and scared, and in some ways that sickness is the worse of the two. Sometimes she wakes up in the middle of the night and thinks about it—wishes she had somebody she could talk to about it or just somebody she could go to the movies with once in a while and share her popcorn with. Heal her, Jesus says.

The fat man in the pickup has a son who is dying. He is dying of AIDS. It was his wife who put the Jesus Loves You sticker on his bumper. The way he sees it, if you don't believe in God anymore, it doesn't make much difference whether Jesus loves you or not. If God lets things happen to people like what has happened to his son, then what is the point of believing in God. Raise him, Jesus says. . . .

We are called by the good God to be the hands and feet and heart of Christ to each other. The church buildings and budgets came later. The forms of church government, the priests and pastors, Baptists and Protestants. The Sunday services with everybody in their best clothes, the Sunday Schools and choirs all came later. So did the Bible study groups and the rummage sales. So did the preachers, the ones on TV who make you sick to your stomach with their phoniness and vulgarity, and the ones closer to home who so often, when I listen to them, seem to proclaim a faith that rarely seems to have much to do either with their own real day-to-day lives in this world or with mine, and the ones also through whose words every once in a while the Word itself touches your heart. They all came later. Maybe the best thing that could happen to the church would be for some great tidal wave of history to wash all that away—the

church buildings tumbling, the church money all lost, the church bulletins blowing through the air like dead leaves, the differences between preachers and congregations all lost too. Then all we would have left would be each other and Christ,

▲ *Standing room only certainly didn't deter J. F. and Diane Winningham from enjoying the Good News that was shared at the Brookwood Baptist Church Easter Sunrise Service in Shreveport, Louisiana.*

Photograph by Jack McCune

137

which was all there was in the first place.

"Truly I say to you, as you did it to the least of these my brethren, you did it to me," Jesus said, which means that in this world now Jesus *is* each other. Heal the sick and be healed. Raise the dead and be raised. Everything that matters comes out of doing those things. Doing those things is what the church is, and when it doesn't do those things, it doesn't matter much what else it does. Preach as you go, saying, "The kingdom of God is at hand," Jesus told the disciples. Be the Kingdom of Heaven. . . .

The Kingdom of Heaven is in the movie theater as the old woman gets up to leave, shaking popcorn crumbs out of her lap. The Kingdom of Heaven is there as the fat man goes driving by in his pickup with the bumper sticker he can't believe in. The Kingdom of Heaven is in the eyes of love and longing and blessing that we raise to look at him as though he was a rainbow in the sky. ‡

‡ *From* The Clown in the Belfry *by Frederick Buechner*

Loving care and encouragement abounds at this Highway ►
and Hedges service. The leadership at Highway and Hedges
Outreach Ministry in Milwaukee, Wisconsin, is comprised
largely of ex-gang members who have committed to
reaching out to gang members and inmates.

Photograph by John J. Korom

▲ A parishioner at Iglesia Resurección Y Vida Central

in Grand Rapids, Michigan, kneels in the pew clutching his

Bible, deep in prayer.

Photograph by David Banta

▲ A survivor of the earthquake in Northridge, California,

spends Sunday in quiet worship in the courtyard of a

Salvation Army community center/shelter in Van Nuys,

California. She believes God placed her there so she could

feel His greatness through the disaster.

Photograph by Tara C. Patty

Simple Goodness

BY JOSEPH CARDINAL BERNARDIN

I have always felt blessed to have come from a loving family, and my heart goes out to those who do not share the same experience. I believe, however, . . . that family goes well beyond blood lines. Family is the human community, the Christian community, and we must learn to love one another as a family. Like any family, we have our disagreements, but in the end we are bonded together.

In the time I was in the hospital recuperating from surgery, and during my subsequent visits for treatments and tests, I have witnessed countless family members and friends caring for a loved one suffering from cancer or other illnesses. I have seen the same resolve on their faces as I had seen on my mother's when she cared for my father, and when she cared for us kids after my father's death. It is tough to watch those we love in pain. But we must believe that by being strong and supportive we make an enormous difference. . . .

I have never felt more like a priest than I have in the past year. Following my first round of chemotherapy and radiation treatments, I told my advisors that I now had a new priority in my ministry: spending time with the sick and the troubled. No matter how significant our other work might be, the people want something different from their clergy. Even if they are not committed to any specific religion, men and women everywhere have a deep desire to come into contact with the transcendent. Members of the clergy can facilitate this through the simple goodness they show in being with their people. The things people are naturally attracted to and remember most are small acts of concern and thoughtfulness. Years later, *that* is what they tell you about their priests and other clergy.

What began as visits to other patients who shared the same floor with me at Loyola Medical Center has since blossomed into a wonderful and life-giving ministry. . . .

Throughout my priesthood, I have always taken seriously my role as one who reaches out to others with compassion and understanding, as one who bears witness to the faith. But I am fully a part of the human community; I am a brother. And because I am a servant of God, I feel much freer to enter into many different communities, each with its own special defining characteristics, and to emphasize solidarity with the much larger human community.

In the light of my cancer ministry, I began to recognize the unique and special nature of another community to which I now belong: the community of those who suffer from cancer and other serious illnesses. Those in this community see things differently. Life takes on new meaning, and suddenly it becomes easier to separate the essential from the peripheral.

As with any community, it is important to share our personal stories, to connect with people, to be understood.

Time and again I have stood in awe as people suffering from life-threatening illnesses have shared with me their insights into life. I have been inspired to see how truly human and how truly wise they are. So often in the past I, like most of us, have struggled with what to say to people who are suffering. But since I was diagnosed as having cancer, words have come much more easily. So has the ability to know when to listen or to simply reach out my hand.

Throughout my own illness I have shared the news about my health as it has been made known to me. My family are the people of metropolitan Chicago—and also of this country and the world. And my family has a right to know how I am doing.

People have told me many times that I am courageous. My decision to discuss my cancer openly and honestly has sent a message that when we are ill, we need not close in on ourselves or remove ourselves from others. Instead, it is during these times when we need people the most.

Some of the media and individuals have also called me a holy man. I do not, however, feel comfortable with this. I have tried to live my life openly and honestly with a deep commitment to the Lord, the Church, and the human community. The past three years have challenged me like never before to hold firm to my beliefs and to trust in the Lord. But my main point has been to put my faith into action, to live out the principles that guide my life. Above all else, I want people to know that I walk with them as their brother, their friend.

My decision to go through my cancer in public has been to share a simple message: Faith really matters. By being grounded in the Lord, by opening myself to his will, I have been able to accept my illness—and now my impending death. What people have seen in the papers or on television has not been a man who wants to look brave or courageous. What they see is a man who believes in God and whose faith informs everything he does. Suffering and pain make little sense to me without God, and my heart goes out to people

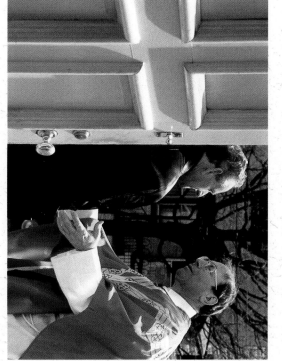

St. John the Baptist Italian Catholic Church in Columbus, Ohio, has a reputation among Italian Americans and with others who share an interest in Italian culture as a place to connect with friends and family. The parish participates in an annual Italian festival, has an extensive library, and offers Italian language classes. Monsignor Mario Serraglio plays an active role in helping to build a sense of community among those who attend St. John's by his personable nature and willingness to be available to those in need.

Photograph by Mark Toro

who feel abandoned or alone in their greatest times of need. As a man of faith, I can really speak of pain and suffering only in terms of their redemptive, salvific qualities. This does not mean I have not prayed, as Jesus did, that it might be God's will that "this cup pass me by." But by embracing the pain, by looking into it and beyond it, I have come to see God's presence in even the worst situations.

Just prior to my surgery, many people asked me to share my thoughts. I said, "I've been a priest for forty-three years and a bishop for twenty-nine of those years. I have always told others to put themselves in the hands of the Lord. I've counseled many people who faced what I am facing. Now it is time to practice what I preach."

During that time I prayed to God for the grace to handle my surgery and postoperative treatment faithfully, without bitterness or undue anxiety. God's special gift to me has been the ability to accept difficult situations, . . . His special gift to me is the gift of peace. ‡

▲ *The final touches are put on a cross in the Field of Hope*

at St. Andrews Presbyterian Church in Austin, Texas.

Following a worship service held to honor the caregivers of

AIDS patients, the congregation moved outside to the Field of

Hope where temporary crosses had been erected, each bearing

the name of someone who had died of AIDS.

Photograph by Kevin Vandivier

‡ *From* The Gift of Peace *by Joseph Cardinal Bernardin*

142

Several Trappist monks rehearse an a cappella chant before ▶

the evening vespers at Our Lady of the Holy Spirit Monastery

in Conyers, Georgia. The monks, who pray unceasingly for

the welfare of the world, welcome priests and lay people alike

in their midst, providing an oasis of peace and

a well spring for spiritual renewal to those who visit.

Photograph by Rob Nelson

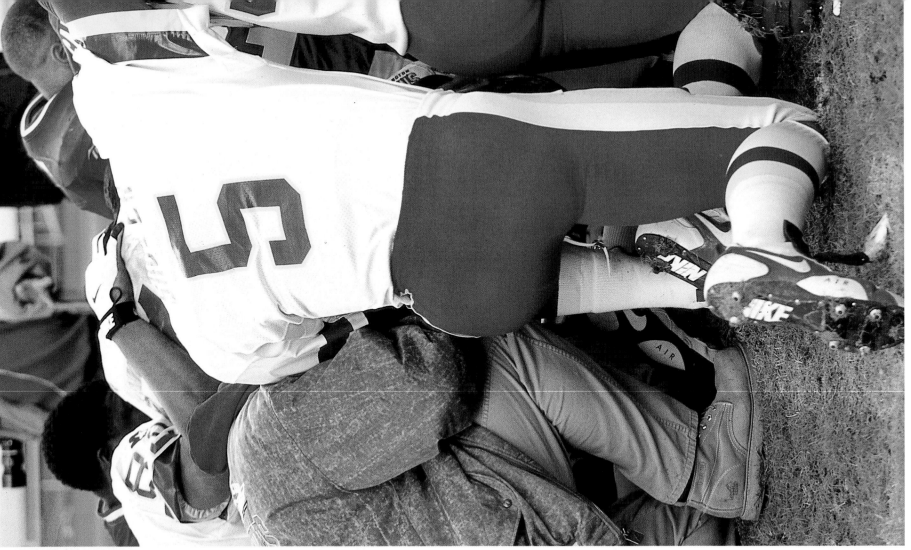

▲ *An usher kneels for the prayer of consecration during Mass at St. Francis Catholic Church in Ann Arbor, Michigan.*

Photograph by Dwight Cendrowski

▲ *The Washington Redskins pray with team members of the New York Giants at the end of an NFL game. Final score: Redskins 31–Giants 21.*

Photograph by Louis DeLuca

▲ *Thousands of junior and senior high school teens from around the nation find fun, friendship, and the answers to their innermost questions at week-long and weekend camps like those offered at Frontier Ranch, a Young Life facility, located in Buena Vista, Colorado.*

Photograph by Gary Christopher

Nikki Lou, Emily Kim, Joy Lee, and Seung Hak Daick celebrate together one Sunday at New Song Community Church, near Los Angeles, California. Younger generations of Asian Americans have found community in churches that embrace a multiethnic presentation, including English services where non-Asians are welcomed. ▲

Photograph by Greg Schneider

147

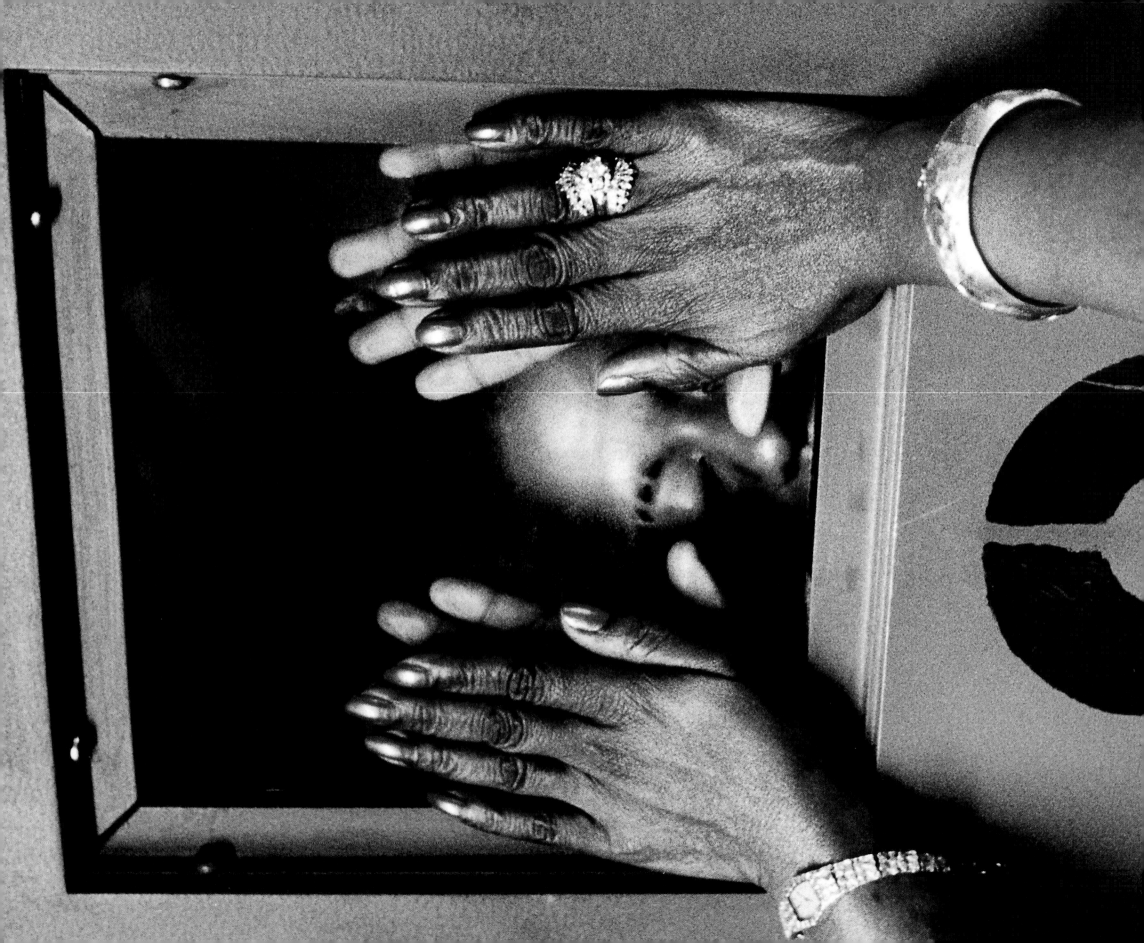

Reaching Out
TO OTHERS

A story is told of a carefree young girl who lived at the edge of a forest, where she loved to play and explore and take long adventurous journeys. But one day she journeyed too deep into the forest and got lost. As the shadows grew long, the girl grew worried. So did her parents. They searched the forest for her, cupping their hands and calling out. But there was no answer. In the gathering night the parents' search grew more intense.

The little girl tried one path after another, but none looked familiar and none led her home. Her skin was welted from the switching of limbs as she pushed her way through the overgrowth. Her knees were scraped from tripping in the dark. Her face was streaked from the tears she had cried. She called for her parents, but the forest seemed to swallow her words. After hours of trying to find her way home, the exhausted girl came to a clearing in the forest, where she curled up on a big rock and fell asleep.

By this time the parents had enlisted the help of friends and neighbors, even strangers from town, to help them search for their lost little girl. In the course of the night many of the searchers went home. But not the girl's father. He searched all night and on into the next morning. In the first light of dawn he spotted his daughter asleep on the rock in the middle of the clearing. He ran as fast as his legs would take him, calling her name. The noise startled the girl awake. She rubbed her eyes. And reaching out to him, she caught his embrace.

"Daddy," she exclaimed, "I found you!"

* * *

He searches for us on the Damascus road or the Emmaus road or whatever road we happen to be traveling at the time, even the pathless road through the forest where we have wandered and ended up lost. He meets us at a rock in the clearing or at a well outside a city in Samaria. He reaches out to us when we're out on a limb in some sycamore tree, the way he did with Zacchaeus, and receives us in the dark, the way he did Nicodemus. He may meet us where we work, charting stars in the heavens, or counting sheep in the fields, or writing study guides in the office. He may meet us in a dream as we sleep or in the Scriptures as we have our morning devotions.

There is no forest so deep that He cannot find us, no night so dark that He cannot see us in all our fears, all our tears, curled up in all our exhaustion. . . . He comes to us where we are, speaks to us in our own language, calls us by our name. ⊹

Bill "The Mailman" Martin delivers his message these days on Sunday—live on KIXL radio in the Austin, Texas area. A retired mail carrier, Bill features gospel music and local black community activities as well as on-air call-in prayer requests from his listeners.

Photograph by Kevin Vandivier

Children of the downtown churches in Franklin, Tennessee, ▲

gather to begin their annual Palm Sunday procession,

which starts at the public library and ends in Franklin

Square, where they participate in a joint worship service.

Photograph by Randy Piland

▲ Ex-gang members respond to a request for prayer from a

young man actively involved in a gang. Outreach to

gang members is a large and important part of the work of

this ministry in Milwaukee, Wisconsin, which

is committed to fighting gang violence through

prayer and discipleship.

Photograph by John J. Korom

Alice Robison loves teaching the kindergarden ▲

children at Pilgrim Congregational United Church of

Christ in Bozeman, Montana. "I learn so much about

myself by the things they say and the questions they ask."

Photograph by Mark MacLeod

▲ Robert and Debbie Mow, members of the deaf ministry at

East Boulder Baptist Church in Lafayette, Colorado, gather

once a month after church for lunch at the Plum Tree

restaurant. Here they discuss the menu while a waitress

stands by to take their order.

Photograph by David Harrison

Christos Arvanitis, an immigrant from Greece, finds the

corner of Graceland and Northwest Highway

in Kenosha, Wisconsin, an opportune spot to share

his message. Christos has mastered his message

in English, often aided by signs he holds high,

even though his native language is Greek.

Photograph by Shawn O'Malley

REACHING OUT

The Change of Heart

BY HENRI J.M. NOUWEN

Jesus does not respond to our worry-filled way of life by saying that we should not be so busy with worldly affairs. He does not try to pull us away from the many events, activities, and people that make up our lives. He does not tell us that what we do is unimportant, valueless, or useless. Nor does he suggest that we should withdraw from our involvements and live quiet, restful lives removed from the struggles of the world.

Jesus' response to our worry-filled lives is quite different. He asks us to shift the point of gravity, to relocate the center of our attention, to change our priorities. Jesus wants us to move from the "many things" to the "one necessary thing." It is important for us to realize that Jesus in no way wants us to leave our many-faceted world. Rather, he wants us to live in it, but firmly rooted in the center of all things. Jesus does not speak about a change of activities, a change in contacts, or even a change of pace. He speaks about a change of heart. This change of heart makes everything different, even while everything appears to be the same. This is the meaning of "Set your hearts on his kingdom first . . . and all these other things will be given you as well." What counts is where our hearts are. When we worry, we have our hearts in the wrong place. . . .

Our lives are destined to become like the life of Jesus. The whole purpose of Jesus' ministry is to bring us to the house of his Father. Not only did Jesus come to free us from the bonds of sin and death, he also came to lead us into the intimacy of his divine life. It is difficult for us to imagine what this means. We tend to emphasize the distance between Jesus and ourselves. We see Jesus as the all-knowing and all-powerful Son of God who is unreachable for us sinful, broken human beings. But in thinking this way, we forget that Jesus came to give us his own life. He came to lift us up into loving community with the Father. Only when we recognize the radical purpose of Jesus' ministry will we be able to understand the meaning of the spiritual life. Everything that belongs to Jesus is given for us to receive. All that Jesus does we may also do. Jesus does not speak about us as second-class citizens. He does not withhold anything from us: "I have made known to you everything I have learned from my Father" (John 15:15); "Whoever believes in me will perform the same works as I do myself" (John 14:12). Jesus wants us to be where he is. In his priestly prayer, he leaves no doubt about his intentions: "Father, may they be one in us, as you are in me and I am in you.... I have given them the glory you gave to me, that they may be one as we are one. With me in them and you in me, may they be so completely one that the world will realize ... that I have loved them as much as you loved me. Father, I want those you have given me to be with me where I am, so that they may always see the glory you have given me.... I have made your name known to them and will continue to make it known, so that the love with which you loved me may be in them, and so that I may be in them" (John 17:21-26).

These words beautifully express the nature of Jesus' ministry. He became like us so that we might become like him. He did not cling to his equality with God but emptied himself and became as we are so that we might become like him and thus share in his divine life....

To be lifted up into the divine life of the Father, the Son, and the Holy Spirit does not mean, however, to be taken out of the world. On the contrary, those who have entered into the spiritual life are precisely the ones who are sent into the world to continue and fulfill the work that Jesus began. The spiritual life does not remove us from the world but leads us deeper into it. Jesus said to his Father, "As you sent me into the world, I have sent them into the world" (John 17:18). He makes it clear that precisely because his disciples no longer belong to the world, they can live in this world as he did: "I am not asking you to remove them from the world, but to protect them from the Evil One. They do not belong to the world any more than I belong to the world" (John 17:15-16). Life in the Spirit of Jesus is therefore a life in which Jesus' coming into the world—his incarnation, his death, and resurrection—is lived out by those who have entered into the same obedient relationship to the Father that marked Jesus' own life. Having become sons and daughters as Jesus was Son, our lives become a continuation of Jesus' mission.

"Being in the world without being in the world." These words summarize well the way Jesus speaks of the spiritual life. ... To live a spiritual life does not mean that we must leave our families, give up our jobs, or change our ways of working; it does not mean that we have to withdraw from social or political activities, or lose interest in literature and art; it does not require severe forms of asceticism or long hours of prayer. Changes such as these may, in fact, grow out of our spiritual life, and for some people radical decisions may be necessary. But the spiritual life can be lived in as many ways as there are people. What is new is that we have moved from the many things to the kingdom of God. What is new is that we are set free from the compulsions of our world and have our hearts set on the only necessary thing. What is new is that we no longer experience the many things, people, and events as endless causes for worry, but begin to experience them as the rich variety of ways in which God makes his presence known to us....

When we set our hearts on the life in the Spirit of Christ, we will come to see and understand better how God keeps us in the palm of his hand. We will come to a better understanding of what we truly need for our physical and mental well-being, and we will come to experience the intimate connections between our spiritual life and our temporal needs while journeying through this world. ‡

‡ From Making All Things New by Henri J. M. Nouwen

▲ Composing his song as he sings it, a member of the

Action Evangelism Team shares his faith on a July

afternoon on the University of California at

Berkeley.

Photograph by Ellen Morrison

Prisoners work hard for the privilege of moving into the ▲

"God Pod" of the Tarrant County Jail in Fort Worth, Texas.

Inmates in this section of the jail must attend Bible studies

and worship services and adhere to strict rules of behavior.

Photograph by Louis DeLuca

◀ *This teen has found a way to communicate an important*

message wherever he goes and whatever he's doing. Even after

dozing off during a late-night program at Greater Love

Tabernacle, in the heart of inner-city Boston, Massachusetts,

the people sitting behind him get his point loud and clear.

Photograph by Dorothy Littell Greco

A man of his word, John Chadwick, pastor of the ▶

Forest Lawn Baptist Church in Balch Springs,

Texas, fulfills a promise to his congregation to

preach from the rooftop when their church's

attendance record was broken.

Photograph by Louis DeLuca

The Nature of Faith

BY JIMMY CARTER

Religious faith has always been at the core of my existence. It has been a changing and evolving experience, beginning when I was a child of three, memorizing verses in Sunday school. When I was nine years old, I was promoted to the Sunday school class taught by my father. . . . My faith at first was simple and unequivocal; there was no doubt in my mind about the truth of what I learned in church.

Yet even as a child, I was dismayed to find myself becoming skeptical about some aspects of my inherited faith. . . . Maybe some Christians never lack faith—they are the lucky ones. However, I don't know of anybody who has never had doubts about any aspect of the Christian faith.

We would like to have an absolutely certain base on which to build our lives—unquestioned faith in everything that the Bible tells us about God, about Jesus, about a quality life, about life after death, about God's love for us. Perhaps we are afraid that opening the door to a little questioning might shake the foundation of our faith or anger God. But I came to realize that it is a mistake not to face our doubts courageously. We should be willing to ask questions, always searching for a closer relationship with God, a more profound faith in Christ. It is foolish to think that our own doubts can change the truth.

When I contemplated abandoning my naval career, I prayed fervently that God would guide me to the right decision. Later, when I lost the 1966 governor's election and was tempted to abandon my faith altogether, my search for God's will sustained me through my anger and disillusionment. I have seen many people with broken lives, some on the verge of alcoholism or even suicide, turn and construct new and vibrant lives based on religious faith. The combined testimonies of countless people with similar experiences have helped to perpetuate religious faith as an integral part of the lives of billions of believers.

Yet the acquiring of faith is not an easy or frivolous thing. How can we prove that God created the universe, that the prophets communicated with God, that Jesus was the Messiah, or that the Resurrection occurred? How can we prove that our lives are meaningful, that truth exists, or that we love or are loved? When I become absorbed in these questions, it helps me to fall back on my faith as a Christian. . . .

My reading of theology, which helped to open these new ideas about faith for me, was an illuminating experience in which I began to feel at ease with my religion for the first time since I was a little child.

I also began to see that my Christian faith and my scientific outlook could be compatible, not conflicting. One of the Bible passages that has helped me understand this is found in Paul's letter to the Romans. Speaking about the pagan peoples of the day, Paul wrote, "That which is known about God is evident within them, for God made it evident to them. For since the creation of the world, His invisible attributes, His eternal power and divine nature, have been clearly seen, being understood through what has been made, so that they are without excuse" (Rom. 1:19-20). Paul's point was that the glories of the world around us prove God's existence.

Like Paul, I see the glory of God around me, in the unfathomable mysteries of the universe and the diversity and intricacies of creation. We stand in wonder at how a tree grows from an acorn, how a flower blooms, or how DNA can shape the appearance and character of a living creature. It is almost humanly incomprehensible that in our Milky Way galaxy there are billions of stars equivalent to our own. At the other end of the scale, I marvel that the inseparable atom I learned about in high school is really a collection of remarkable components, matter and antimatter, rotating in different directions yet held together by forces of immense power, and some particles able to pass through the entire earth without being deflected.

Even more miraculous is the human form, in which the trillions of neuron connections in a single human brain exceed the total number of celestial bodies in the known heavens! Scientific knowledge only enhances my sense of God's glory filling the universe. Over the centuries, scientists have discovered more and more about these truths—truths that have always existed. None of these discoveries contradicts my belief in an ultimate and superior being; they simply confirm the reverence and awe generated by what becomes known and what remains unexplained. . . .

In its own way, technology offers a lesson in the nature of faith. Aren't there plenty of things in modern life that we believe but can't understand? The computer, radio, television, space travel—all once seemed miraculous, but most of us now accept them as routine. We can set up an antenna and bring in 150 different television programs. The waves are all around us, plus countless radio signals, waiting for us to extract them from the ether for our pleasure or information. There is no way for us to detect in advance that the signals are here, or for most of us to explain how these electromagnetic waves can be changed into music or colored, moving pictures almost instantaneously. These are amazing things that few of us comprehend, but we believe them.

In the same way, I cannot fully understand many religious concepts, even some aspects of the life of Christ—the extremes of love and judgment, power and weakness, the demand for perfection and total forgiveness, the omnipotence of God and his human Son weeping and tempted. The totality of it is overwhelming, but I accept it with confidence—through faith.

In addition to the intellectual realization of a supreme being, we have a purely subjective need to meet a personal yearning. We have an innate desire to relate to the all-knowing, the all-powerful, and the ever-present—to some entity that transcends ourselves. I am grateful and happy when I feel the presence of God within me, as a tangible influence on my thoughts and on the ultimate standards of my life. It is reassuring to me to know that God will always be with me and cares for me. I think of the words of Isaiah: "When you pass through the waters, I will be with you; and through the rivers, they shall not overwhelm you; when you walk through fire you shall not be burned, and the flame shall not consume you. For I am the Lord your God. . . . You are precious in my sight, and honored, and I love you" (Isa. 43:2–4).

Our Sunday school class often becomes involved in a discussion about how to achieve this closeness to God. Except in moments of crisis, when we reach desperately for some sustaining force, the relationship requires some effort on our part, some reaching out. I remind my class of the man in terrible trouble who prayed, "God, if you'll just get me out of this mess, I promise never to bother you with my prayers again." We need God's presence at all times—not just when life is at its most difficult. . . . Our faith should be a guide for us in deciding between the permanent and the transient, the important and the insignificant, the gratifying and the troubling, the joyful and the depressing. . . .

Of course, the fellowship of faith is even larger than the Christian world. The first great Christian theologian, Paul, repeatedly emphasized the fundamental importance of faith as a unifying force between Christians and Jews. A burning question in the early church was whether God's covenant with Abraham was exclusively for the Jews. Some feared that if they became Christians they would forgo God's blessing. Paul made it clear that it was the patriarch's faith and not his ethnicity that was significant. He relied on the Scripture: "For the promise that he should be the heir of the world was not to Abraham or to his seed, through the law, but through the righteousness of faith" (Rom. 4:13). The covenant with God is shared by Jews and Christians, with faith in one God as the unifying element. . . .

When people become alienated from one another, it is important to search for a healing force. A husband and wife may have a child who can hold them together. Members of an athletic team who don't really like one another will cooperate in the heat of a game. Our faith in God should play such a unifying role among believers. This may seem obvious, but all too often we forget or ignore it.

Christians of various denominations and shades of practice should emphasize shared concepts that are so great and so important that, compared with them, other differences fade into relative insignificance. Our faith should transcend all merely human issues, such as whether we are immersed or sprinkled in baptism, have few or many ordinances, have servant pastors or a hierarchical church with bishops and maybe a pope. We can rise above all this when we come together as common believers, but doing so requires both an elevation in spirit and a degree of personal humility. . . . *Church* does not mean just. . . . "Baptist" or "Protestant"; it is the totality of those united in the love of Christ. The ultimate vision of the church should be as a worldwide community in which all believers are joined. As I have come to know, reaching out to others in the name of God can be one of the most deeply rewarding experiences any person can enjoy. ‡

‡ *From* Living Faith *by Jimmy Carter*

Photograph by Jay Janner

Contributors

PHOTOGRAPHY

Wende Alexander Clark is a photojournalist on hiatus from the *Grand Rapids Press*. She won several national and state awards for documenting a women's drug rehab center in Bridgeport, CT, and has won various state awards for her work in Michigan. Wende lives with her husband and two children in Comstock Park, MI.

Andres R. Alonso is a photojournalist whose photographs have appeared in *The Washington Post*, *USA Today*, *Outside Magazine*, and *The New York Times*. Andres resides with his wife and two children in Roanoke, VA.

Peggy Bair is a photographer for the *St. Joseph News-Press*. She graduated from the University of Missouri at Kansas City in 1986. Peggy makes her home with her husband in Leavenworth, KS.

Lee Balgemann has worked in his own studio since 1982 after thirteen years as a photo editor for the Chicago bureau of The Associated Press. Lee, his wife, and two sons live in River Forest, IL.

David Banta is an assignment photojournalist and commercial photographer. He attended the Institute of Design at the Illinois Institute of Technology and holds a degree in Arts and Media from William James College. David lives with his wife in Grand Rapids, MI.

Dave Bartruff is an award-winning photographer who has traveled to over eighty countries. He is the leading photographic contributor to the 1997 UNICEF World Calendar. Dave and his wife attend the First Presbyterian Church of San Rafael, and reside in San Anselmo, CA.

James Edward Bates is a photojournalist who completed his degree in advertising before identifying photography as his true calling. He is now enrolled in photojournalism courses at University of Southern Mississippi. James makes his home in Ocean Springs, MS.

David Bell is a freelance photographer whose assignments have taken him to Europe and the Middle East. He has been a staff member of Southwestern Baptist Seminary and a photography instructor at North Arkansas Community College. David lives with his wife and two of his three children in Berryville, AR.

Louis Bencze is a photographer who specializes in corporate literature and advertising. His clients include Pacific Telecom, Port of Vancouver, Santa Fe Railway, Anheuser-Busch, and Federal Express. Louis lives with his wife and three children in Brush Prairie, OH.

"Taking photographs for the Sunday in America book project surprised and delightened me with more rewards than I ever expected. . . .

After choosing to photograph . . . St. John The Baptist Italian Catholic Church with its ethnic charm and warm community spirit, I immediately felt the return of something special. . . . I began to feel, for the first time since my childhood, a welcome back to my home culture."
—Mark Toro

Brian Branch-Price is a staff photographer for the *Wilmington News Journal*. He graduated from Howard University in 1991 and won a National Headliner first place award for sports in 1995. Brian has five sons and lives in Wilmington, DE.

Walter Calahan is a freelance photographer who has enjoyed taking photos since he was a Cub Scout. His images have appeared in Boy Scout magazines *Boys Life* and *Exploring*, as well as in *USA Today*, *National Geographic World*, *TIME*, and *Newsweek*. Walter lives with his wife in Arlington, VA.

Dwight Cendrowski is a photographer who has done freelance work since 1978. He has worked for a wide variety of corporate and editorial clients, combining his photojournalism background and lighting expertise. Dwight lives with his wife and children in Ann Arbor, MI.

Gus Chan is a staff photographer for the *Cleveland Plain Dealer*. He recently completed a book project with twenty other Ohio photographers entitled *A Day at Jacobs Field*. Gus lives with his wife and five daughters in Cleveland Heights, OH.

Gary Christopher is a photographer whose career has spanned over thirty years. In recent years he has turned his talents toward creating artistic scenics. Gary makes his home in Beaumont, TX.

Al Cook creates multi-image/multimedia productions for church and mission efforts. He also produces book covers and multiple lines of greeting cards. Al resides with his wife and two children in Lanexa, VA.

Alan Craft is a photographer with sixteen years of experience in editorial and advertising photography. He has more than 100 magazine, annual reports, and book covers to his credit. Alan lives with his wife and son in Tacoma, WA.

Pat Davison is a photojournalist who won a Distinguished Service Award from the Society of Professional Journalists for a series on the threat to wildlife spurred by the booming demand for elk products. Pat lives with his wife and two children in Westminster, CO.

James D. DeCamp is a freelance photographer who started out as a stringer for Cincinatti newspapers during his teen years and has been recognized by several news and photography associations. James lives with his wife and two daughters in Reynoldsburg, OH.

Louis DeLuca is a staff photographer for the *Dallas Morning News*, who has been named National Press Photographers' Association Regional Photographer of the Year four times. Louis, his wife, and two children live in Dallas, TX.

John de Visser is a photojournalist who has worked for several prominent editorial, corporate, and governmental clients throughout his thirty-year career. He has won the National Film Board Gold Medal for Still Photography as well as Art Directors Awards in the US and Canada. John makes his home in Cobourg, Ontario, Canada.

Gary Fong is the Director of Editorial Graphics Technology at the *San Francisco Chronicle*. He has taught photography and photojournalism at University of California, Berkeley and San Francisco State University, respectively. Gary resides in Castro Valley, CA.

Pam Francis is a photographer who takes pictures for magazines and advertising agencies. She was a graphic designer until the age of thirty-four, when she realized that photo shoots were the favorite part of her job. Pam lives with her husband in Houston, TX.

Gibbs Frazeur is a freelance photographer who has worked for several daily newspapers and attended the Master's Program at the School of Visual Communication at Ohio University in Athens, Ohio. Gibbs attends the Louisville Mennonite Fellowship with his wife and four sons in Louisville, KY.

3/16/97 Our Lady of Mt. Carmel. Arrive at 10 A.M. for Mass. Too late! Everyone else is already there. I've never been to Mass before. Watch. Do not take photos. After service, photograph Msgr. shaking hands with parishioners. It's very cold. My new camera battery dies after 5 shots and I don't have another. Embarrassed.

3/23/97 Palm Sunday. Wonderful service. Everyone is so generous and receptive even though they don't know who I am. . . . Spend most of time listening to service. Am moved by people's faith. Feel guilty. Everyone is praying for salvation; I'm praying for good shots.

After service, taxi over to the First Spanish Presbyterian Church of Brooklyn, my friend Elizabeth's church. Service is in a small chapel. Love the intimacy. . . . The room is filled with faith and love. Everywhere I look I see pictures. I'm in heaven!

3/24/97 I'm sick. . . . Can't get sick now; Easter is coming. . . .

3/30/97 Easter Sunday. Everyone tells me to stay home and rest. Not photograph Easter Sunday? I have to go! . . . Arrive at Our Lady of Mt. Carmel Church. See photos immediately. Great shot on church steps. Take some photos in church but it's hard. The church is filled to capacity. All the seats are taken.

and the aisles are filled. I'm weak and there's no place to sit. I see a great shot at the altar. Nobody is looking that way right this minute. I ask the usher if he thinks the shot's OK. "I think that would be pushing it," he says. What was I thinking? Maybe I'm delirious.

4/5/97 Rock Mass. Saturday night, not Sunday. Who'll know! Trip over thing you kneel on and am sent flying.... Problems with flash, hardly anything comes out. Shouldn't have taken photos on Saturday! Jinxed!

4/6/97-10 AM Our Lady of Mt. Carmel. I find myself singing along with "Holy! Holy! Holy!" Have been singing it all week. Find myself saying "Amen" after prayers. Maybe that's why people in both churches think I'm going to convert to Christianity. See children in beautiful white clothes. Photograph them. Return to service. Am unexpectedly sprinkled with holy water. Instinctively duck. What must the priest think of me! Special baptism. No wonder the children were dressed in white. Get the shot.
—Ethel Wolvovitz

2 PM Our Lady of Mt. Carmel Church. Return to church to photograph other baptisms. Everyone is so nice to me even though I'm sure I'm in their way. That must be what it means to be a good Christian....
—Ethel Wolvovitz

Doug Hopfer is a freelance editorial and commercial photographer who has worked on several international documentary projects for mission groups.

Rina Ganassa photographs weddings, portraits, and commercial subjects. She graduated with honors from Brooks Institute of Photography in 1989 and now makes her home in Santa Barbara, CA.

John Godbey is a photographer for the *Decatur Daily*. He has received awards from the Alabama Press Association and the Alabama Associated Press. John lives with his wife and two daughters in Decatur, AL.

Bob Greenlee is a photography instructor at Hannibal LaGrange College and a part-time photographer for the *Hannibal Courier-Post* newspaper. Bob and his wife attend Immanuel Baptist Church in Hannibal, MO.

Bob Hagle is the Manager of Employee Communications for Lord Corporation. He earned his MFA in Visual Communications from Syracuse University and has compiled his images in a stock photo collection. Bob and his wife live in Erie, PA.

Rick Harrig owns a commercial photography studio, having worked as a medical illustrator for the Air Force and as art director and photographer for various ad agencies. Rick makes his home in Omaha, NE.

David Harrison is a staff photographer at the *Topeka Capital-Journal* who pursued a career in auto racing before graduating from the University of Colorado's Journalism School. David lives with his wife and five children in Wheaton, IL.

Craig Lee is a staff photographer for the *San Francisco Examiner*. He has won awards from the National Press Photographers Association and the Associated Press. Craig is a 1983 graduate of San Jose State University and resides in San Francisco, CA.

Greg Lehman is a photojournalist for the *Walla Walla Union-Bulletin*. He left the radio industry for photography over thirteen years ago and lives with his wife and step-children in Walla Walla, WA.

Jean-Claude Lejeune is a freelance photographer. He won the Grand Prize awarded by the French Federation of Postcard Publishers in 1996. Jean-Claude lives with his wife and child in LA.

Jack McCune is a freelance photographer. He began his photography career in 1988, when he photographed the Winter Olympics in Calgary, Canada, as well as the Superbowl. Jack lives with his wife and son in Shreveport, LA.

David Jenkins is a photographer and author of *Rock City Barns: A Passing Era*. His photographs have appeared in *TIME*, *Omni*, *Moody*, and the *Philadelphia Inquirer* Sunday Magazine. Dave and his wife attend the First Presbyterian Church in Chattanooga, TN.

William Koechling is a freelance photographer who graduated from Wheaton College in 1972. He has done editorial and advertising photography for L.L. Bean, The Eaton Corporation, and Christianity Today, Inc. William resides with his wife and five children in Wheaton, IL.

John J. Korom is the head photographer at Pohlman Advertising Photography Studios. He has taught photographic lighting and photojournalism at Milwaukee Area Technical College, where he was a graduate in 1982. John lives with his wife and two children in Wauwatosa, WI.

James Frederick Housel is a photographer who divides his time between commercial photography and volunteer work with CARE, the world's largest private relief and development organization. James lives with his wife and two children in Seattle, WA.

Jay Janner is a photographer for *The Gazette*. He graduated from Texas A&M University in 1991 and was named Texas Photographer of the Year in 1993 by the Headliners Foundation of Texas. He lives with his wife and two daughters in Colorado Springs, CO.

Dorothy Littel Greco is a photojournalist who works for corporate, editorial, and nonprofit organizations. She specializes in environmental portraits. Dorothy attends the Vineyard Christian Fellowship and lives with her husband and two sons in Jamaica Plain, MA.

Ron Londen is a partner with Journey Communications, a publishing firm. Before working with Journey, he was director of photography at the *Orange County Register* in southern California. Ron lives with his wife and three daughters in Charlottesville, VA.

Mark MacLeod specializes in commercial and fine art photography of the American West. For three months in 1996 and 1997, he was the guest artist at the Montana Governor's mansion. As a third generation Montanan, Mark makes his home in Bozeman, MT.

Randy Mallory is a freelance photographer and writer who regularly contributes to *Texas Highways*, the official state travel magazine. He has worked in fields ranging from travel to medical to industrial. Randy lives with his wife and two children in Tyler, TX.

Matthew Lester works as a freelance photographer and photojournalist. He recently graduated from Baylor University, where he worked on a photo documentary project on the Branch Davidian survivors four years after the ATF raid at Mt. Carmel. Matthew lives in Denver, CO.

Michael Lewis is a freelance photojournalist who worked as a print and broadcast journalist. He is the principal photographer for a magazine published by the Church of the Nazarene and regularly shoots assignments for *TIME* and *Newsweek*. Michael lives with his wife in Denver, CO.

"Said Jesus, 'The poor you will always have with you . . .' (Mark 14:7). What good is it, my brothers, if a man claims to have faith but has no deeds?

What struck me when I first began photographing the Storehouse was . . . that I was witnessing, photographing, a minute cross-section of an immense picture spanning the nation. Unending is the stream of have-nots. The image repeats itself each morning when the doors of the Storehouse, like the arms of Jesus, open to receive those our society has nearly forgotten. If the tiny amount of photographic talent I freely give improves, in some unseen way, the life of a person I shall never know then Thy will is being done."
—Jonathan A. Meyers

Ron Londen *(Wrote James (2:14), "What good is it . . .")*

Paula Nelson is the Senior Staff Photographer and Photo Editor for the *Dallas Morning News*. She won a Pulitzer Prize in 1994 for a report on violence against women in India and Thailand. Paula makes her home in Dallas, TX.

Rob Nelson works as a contract photographer for Black Star, Inc., where he covers news and feature stories throughout the South for *Newsweek*, *TIME*, *The New York Times*, and several regional magazines. Nelson lives with his wife and son in Woodstock, GA.

He graduated with a photography and business degree from East Texas State University. Doug, his wife, and his four children worship at The Father's House in Garland, TX.

Jonathan Meyers is a freelance photographer and writer whose photo stories have appeared in over thirty countries. Jonathan has made his home in New Mexico for twenty-three years and currently resides with his wife and daughter in Albuquerque, NM.

Doug Milner was a photojournalist who worked for the *Dallas Times Herald* for seven years before turning to freelance work. His work has appeared in *Newsweek*, *Fortune*, *Sports Illustrated*, and *Entertainment Weekly*. Doug passed away in November of 1995 and is survived by a wife and daughter who live in Terrell, TX.

Ellen Morrison is a freelance photographer for the *Roseville California Press Tribune*. She received a degree in photography from Sierra College in Rocklin and strives to "capture a moment in time" with her camera. Ellen lives with her husband in Auburn, CA.

Ron Nickel is a self-taught freelance photographer. He produces images that are regularly published in *Campus Life Magazine* and has won several Evangelical Press Association awards. Ron resides with his wife and two children in Three Hills, Alberta, Canada.

Shawn O'Malley is a corporate and editorial photographer. He is currently a staff photographer and photo editor at the Allstate Insurance Company. Shawn lives with his wife and three children in Kenosha, WI.

Tara Patty is a documentary photographer who has produced essays on AIDS care in Africa, survivors of the 1994 Northridge earthquake, and a children's hospital in Haiti. Tara is a member of the National Press Photographers Association and Christians in Photojournalism, and makes her home in Chaska, MN.

Robert Pavuchak is a photographer for the *Pittsburgh Post Gazette*. He has won numerous awards from photographer associations and is the current historian of the Photographers Association of Greater Pittsburgh, where he is a past president and the first Photographer of the Year. Robert lives with his wife in West Mifflin, PA.

Angela Peterson is a general assignment photographer for the *Orlando Sentinel*. She has produced several traveling exhibits that reflect the culture and heritage of African-Americans from the Central Florida communities. Angela makes her home in Orlando, FL.

Bill Petros is a photojournalist and commercial photographer who belongs to the White House News Photographers Association. He is the father of three children and lives in Washington, D. C.

Randy Piland is senior staff photographer for the *Tennessean*. He served as an Army photojournalist in the National Guard and was deployed to the Middle East to cover the Gulf War. Randy has two children and lives with his wife in Nashville, TN.

Mark Richards is a freelance photographer who has worked for such publi-

cations as *TIME*, *The New York Times Magazine*, *Newsweek*, *Fortune*, *Business Week* and *Parenting*. Mark lives with his wife and two children in Mill Valley, CA.

Michael Schimpf is a freelance photographer who travels extensively for corporate, editorial, and travel/leisure clients. He is currently working on a personal project on the people of Madagascar. Michael lives in Lansing, MI.

Greg Schneider is a freelance photographer who has twice been named California Press Photographer of the Year. From 1980 to 1993, he documented the missions of Campus Crusade for Christ throughout five dozen countries. Greg lives with his wife and daughter in Redlands, CA.

Robert Seale is a staff photographer at *The Sporting News* in St Louis, Missouri. He is a graduate from Stephen F. Austin State University and lives with his wife in Houston, TX.

Karim Shamsi-Basha is a freelance photojournalist who has worked for *TIME*, *LIFE*, and *Newsweek*. He has done freelance work for nine years and regularly shoots for *Sports Illustrated*. Karim lives with his wife and two sons in Birmingham, AL.

Bruce C. Strong is a photographer for the *Orange County Register*. He has won numerous awards, including the California Press Photographer of the Year. He lives with his wife in Orange, CA

Mark Toro is an editorial freelance

photographer. He is the winner of numerous awards and a graduate of Ohio Institute of Photography. Mark and his wife make their home in Columbus, OH.

Walt Unks works as a staff photographer for the *Durham Herald-Sun*. After graduating in 1988 from Ohio University with a BFA in Visual Communications, he worked as a staff photographer at the *Augusta Chronicle*. Walt lives with his wife in Durham, NC.

Jerry Valente is a freelance corporate and editorial photographer who has participated in several Day in the Life projects. He had two winning entries in the 48th Annual Pictures of the Year Competition. Jerry makes his home in Boston, MA.

Dewey Vanderhoff is a freelance photographer who divides his work between photojournalism and commercial illustration. He is based near Yellowstone National Park and has been photographing American West subjects for over twenty-five years. Dewey resides in Cody, WY.

Doug Van De Zande is a commercial photographer whose assignments include advertising, architectural, portraiture, and annual report work. He graduated from Brooks Institute in 1979. Doug lives with his wife and two children in Raleigh, NC.

Kevin Vandivier is a freelance photographer who began his career in 1982 at the *Dallas Times Herald*. His work has been published in many magazines, including *LIFE*, *Newsweek*, *TIME*, and

National Geographic World Magazine. Kevin lives with his wife and four children in Austin, TX.

Tom Watson is a corporate photographer who has traveled on assignment throughout the world. He enjoys white water kayaking, skiing, and all water sports with his family. Tom lives with his wife and two sons on Skaneateles Lake, NY.

Mark Williams is a freelance photographer and former staffer with the *Dallas Times Herald*. His clients include *USA Today*, *GTE*, and Southwest Airlines. He studied photojournalism at the University of North Texas in Denton. Mark lives with his wife in Flower Mound, TX.

Nita Winter is a freelance photographer who specializes in creating emotion-evoking images of people in real life situations. Her multi-cultural images have illustrated several books and the Children's Defense Fund calendar for the past five years. Nita makes her home in San Francisco, CA.

Don Wolf is a forty-two-year veteran of commercial and editorial photography. He enjoys showing slides of his trips to Croatia to raise funds for an orphanage located there. Don has five children and lives with his wife in Kansas City, KS.

Ethel Wolvovitz is a first grade teacher whose photographs have appeared in magazines and museums. Until this assignment, she had never attended a church service. Ethel lives in Brooklyn, NY.

> *"My life will never be the same. The opportunity to photograph for Sunday in America led me to Highway and Hedges Outreach Ministries. I've questioned whether the skills God gave me would ever glorify Jesus Christ. By seeing God's work in action, I now know He does answer prayer. . . It was not a coincidence that my name was picked for this project. . . .*
>
> *—John J. Korom*

> *I've realized I'm just like a preacher with a camera. My camera is a tool to help other people see the passion Jesus has for his people—and the freedom and passion some people have for Jesus. Pictures are like jewels of color crystalized as a permanent record for others to see.*
>
> *—Doug Hopfer*

ESSAYS

© 1996 by Kelly K. Monroe. Reprinted in the abridged form by permission of Zondervan Publishing House. (p. 9)

Bernardin, Joseph Cardinal. Excerpt from *The Gift of Peace*. Loyola Press, Chicago, Illinois. Copyright © 1997 by Catholic Bishop of Chicago, a Corporation Sole. Reprinted in the abridged form by permission of Loyola Press. (p. 140)

Buechner, Frederick. Excerpt from Chapter 13, "The Church" from *The Clown in the Belfry: Writings on Faith and Fiction*. HarperSan Francisco, San Francisco, California. Copyright © 1992 by Frederick Buechner. Reprinted in the abridged form by permission of HarperCollins Publishers, Inc. (p. 134)

Carter, Jimmy. Excerpt from *Living Faith*. Random House, New York. Copyright © 1996 by Jimmy Carter. Reprinted in the abridged form by permission of Random House, Inc. (p. 162)

Dole, Elizabeth. "Crisis and Faith." Taken from *In Finding God at Harvard*, edited by Kelly Monroe. Zondervan Publishing House, Grand Rapids, Michigan. Copyright

Evan, Tony. Excerpt from *Our God is an Awesome God*, Moody Press, Chicago, Illinois. Copyright © 1994 by Anthony T. Evans. Reprinted in the abridged form by permission of Moody Press. (p. 42)

Gire, Ken. Excerpt from *Windows of the Soul*, Zondervan Publishing House. Grand Rapids, Michigan. Copyright © 1996 by Ken Gire, Jr. Reprinted in the abridged form by permission of Zondervan Publishing House. (pp. 35, 69, 101, 125, 149)

Norris, Kathleen. Excerpt "Getting To Hope," from *Dakota: A Spiritual Geography*. Ticknor & Fields, New York, New York. Copyright © 1993 by Kathleen Norris. Reprinted in the abridged form by permission of Ticknor & Fields/Houghton Mifflin Company. All rights reserved. (p. 92)

Nouwen, Henri J. M. Excerpt from pages 41-61 from *Making All Things New: An Invitation to the Spiritual Life*. Harper SanFrancisco, California. Reprinted in the abridged form by permission of HarperCollins Publishers, Inc. (p. 156)

Stafford, Tim. *Knowing the Face of God*. NavPress, Colorado Springs, Colorado. Copyright © by Tim Stafford. Excerpt reprinted in the abridged form by permission of NavPress. For copies call 1-800-366-7788. (p. 80)

Tada, Joni Eareckson. "Seeking God With Specific Requests" from *Seeking God: My Journey of Prayer and Praise*. Wolgemuth & Hyatt Publishers, Brentwood, Tennessee. Copyright © 1991 by Joni Eareckson Tada. Book is now titled *A Quiet Place in a Crazy World*. Questar Publishers, Inc., Sisters, Oregon. Rights held by JAF Ministries, Agoura Hills, California. Excerpt reprinted in the abridged form by permission of JAF Ministries. (p. 54)

Wangerin Jr., Walter. Excerpt from pages 3-6 from *Ragman and Other Cries of Faith*. HaperSanFrancisco, San Francisco, California. Copyright © 1984 by Walter Wangerin, Jr. Reprinted in the abridged form by permission of HarperCollins Publishers, Inc. (p. 120)

Yancy, Phillip. Excerpt from *I was just Wondering*, William B. Eerdmans Publishing Company, Grand Rapids, Michigan. Copyright © 1989 by Wm. B. Eerdmans Publishing Co. Reprinted in the abridged form by permission of Wm. B. Eerdmans Publishing Co. (p. 112)

Yancy, Phillip. Excerpt from *Finding God in Unexpected Places*. Moorings, A Division of the Ballantine Publishing Group, Random House, Inc. Nashville, Tennessee. Copyright © 1995 by Phillip Yancey. Reprinted in the abridged form by permission of Ballantine Books, A Division of Random House, Inc. (pp. 112-114)

168